Under a Pink Sky

*A mother's story of love, loss
and the power of forgiveness*

ESTHER GHEY

with Gay Longworth

MICHAEL  JOSEPH

PENGUIN MICHAEL JOSEPH

UK | USA | Canada | Ireland | Australia
India | New Zealand | South Africa

Penguin Michael Joseph is part of the Penguin Random House group of companies
whose addresses can be found at global.penguinrandomhouse.com.

Penguin Random House UK, One Embassy Gardens, 8 Viaduct Gardens, London SW11 7BW

penguin.co.uk

First published 2025

001

Set in 12.5/14.75pt Garamond MT Std
Typeset by Penguin Books
Printed and bound in Great Britain by Clays Ltd, Elcograf S.p.A.

The authorized representative in the EEA is Penguin Random House Ireland,
Morrison Chambers, 32 Nassau Street, Dublin D02 YH68.

A CIP catalogue record for this book is available from the British Library.

HARDBACK ISBN: 978–0–241–73873–3
TRADE PAPERBACK ISBN: 978–1–405–97426–4

Penguin Random House is committed to a sustainable future for our
business, our readers and our planet. This book is made from
Forest Stewardship Council® certified paper.

Under a Pink Sky

For Brianna x

Contents

Prologue

So, Tell Me, What Was Brianna Like?

Laura Kuenssberg wasn't the first to ask me that question. I am almost always asked what Brianna was like when I am being interviewed and it always gives me this startling milli-second of a moment that makes me feel I no longer know where I am in the world. It is like the moment when I wake up each morning and open my eyes to the unbearable truth that I must survive in a world in which my child has been murdered. So, tell me, what was Brianna like? It is not only the past tense in that question that catches me, it is the enormity of it as well. The universe blinks, a vastness opens up and I teeter on the edge of the black hole that sits deep in my heart . . . but I breathe and I focus and I force my feet to feel the floor and I start to respond. How-ever many times I have managed to pull a reply out of my broken heart, I have never yet been able to fully answer it. I know what I've said in a multitude of interviews. And I know what I haven't.

I

I've said . . .

She was absolutely full of life.
She was such a character.
She was really outgoing.
She was strikingly beautiful.
She was strong.
She was witty.
She was sassy. As hell!
She loved to be on TikTok.
She loved the likes.
She brushed off the hate.
She was the life and soul of the party.
She was unforgettable.
She loved attention.
She was sharp-tongued.
She was fierce.
She was fearless.
She was a good listener.
She loved her pink fluffy pyjamas.
She loved the dogs.
She was perfectly manicured to the very tips
    of her exceptionally long nails.
She was one of a kind.
She was flamboyant.
She was fashionable.

All of those answers are true. But they are not the whole truth. It is important that we don't speak ill of the dead, but it is equally important that we don't see them only through rose-tinted glasses, because to understand Brianna's death, you must understand her life. It is, I am sorry to say, also true that my 'fashionable, flamboyant' child sometimes wouldn't tidy her room and lived in squalor and filth. Sometimes my 'strikingly beautiful' baby wouldn't brush her teeth for days. The 'perfectly mani-cured' Brianna sometimes refused to wash. The 'outgoing' Brianna sometimes couldn't leave the house. The 'life and soul of the party' spent her last Christmas alone. The 'fear-less' Brianna had never, until the day she was killed, taken a bus on her own, and yet she would walk the halls of school resplendent in a wig, false eyelashes, painted talons, live-streaming on her beloved pink phone, talking back to anyone who told her she couldn't.

Someone sent a friend of hers a text asking: who is this Brianna, strutting around the school as if she owns the place? Who indeed.

Brianna was born on 7 November 2006. She was not given the name Brianna when I gave birth to her. In fact, she was named Brett, she was my second child and she was a boy. I know that is incredibly hard for some to comprehend, and I understand that. I do. However, for me, for us as a family, who knew and loved her deeply and unconditionally, when the transition happened for Brianna it was perhaps one of the easiest parts of her short life. That is not to say transitioning is uncomplicated, but as you will read in the pages of this book, Brianna's took place within a maelstrom of mental health problems, isolation, anxiety, an eating disorder, bouts of self-harm and a chronic screen addiction, so from my perspective as her mother, Brett becoming Brianna was the most positive part of that troubled time.

I am only telling this story because she cannot, so I am extremely aware of the need to get this right. I can feel her standing just behind me, tapping her acrylics impatiently.

'Like, literally!'

I also know I will not succeed. Parents rarely get it right, have you noticed that? What I will try to do is tell *my* story without making assumptions about hers. I know that for sixteen years I loved, parented and cared for my child who for fourteen years we called Brett, who will forever be known as Brianna, but who we at home mostly called Bree. Names matter, and I will give due diligence to the name Brianna chose for herself, but it is important to me, as her mother, that I am able to remember and mourn the child I gave birth to on 7 November 2006 just as much as the child who was murdered on 11 February 2023. My beautiful daughter was killed and is dead. I don't know if I will ever truly absorb that fact, as fact. She was part of me. She is still part of me. I can count on two hands the times when we did not sleep under the same roof from the day she was born. Walking past her bedroom night after night is the hardest part of my day. Where is she? Why is she not here playing music, making those extremely annoying TikTok videos or lying in the garden playing with the dogs, cracking jokes in silly voices? Why isn't she here slouching around the living room with her sister in the pink fluffy pyjamas she loved so much I gave them to the undertakers so they could dress her in them? Why can she no longer turn the camera on herself and perform to the crowd? 'Here I am!' was one of her megaphone announcements, her verbal calling card. So why isn't she here? That is just as difficult a question to answer. But for my own peace of mind, I am going to try.

In my comments to the court, I said, and I still feel, that I lost them both, Brett and Brianna, and now all that remains of my child are ashes in a box. There is small comfort that the box is decorated with pink clouds and rests with us at home in her room that we have redecorated since her death – pink, of course – but it's a very small comfort compared to the gaping hole that huge personality has left behind. In writing my story I do not want to upset anyone, but, pronouns aside, ashes are all that is left of my child. Yes, names matter, they absolutely do and gender matters, it absolutely does. But so do memories.

When Brett was little, he was utterly joyful, mischievous, exuberant and never sat still. He always wanted to be outside, on the beach, by the lake, the park, anywhere where there was space to accommodate his apparent limitless energy. If you couldn't see him – because he was often cartwheeling off in the opposite direction – you could hear him. He commanded my attention. If he bumped into friends, it was as if a firework had gone off. Uncontainable glee would explode. At primary school there was space for the backflips and gymnastics that he excelled at, but when he went to secondary school, when he was given his first phone, when there were stricter rules to follow, some of that glee started to slip away. At home he was, as ever, the cheeky monkey I had always known him to be, but as adolescence accelerated towards us, he got into more and more trouble. By the age of thirteen he was so disruptive at school it was strongly suggested, and I agreed, that he would be better off somewhere else. Apart from flashes of his old self, I felt like I was losing my child. Like many teens, he was already pushing me away, and when Covid-19 happened, life as we all knew it changed overnight. The online world that Brett disappeared into caused untold amounts of harm. However, and this is why this story is so complex, out of the murky cocoon of lockdown a beautiful bright pink butterfly emerged, and she was called Brianna. I miss her so much it hurts.

So, what was Brianna like?

Well, I can tell you one thing for certain, she was, she still is, the star of the show.

I

Pick Your Battles

Pick your battles: that's what they say when you become a parent. Pick your battles. Brianna and I had so many battles: attitude, phone use, tidying up after herself, screen time, the way she spoke to me, going to school – that was a big one – the clothes she wore, the videos she made, the things she posted, the people she followed. Sometimes it felt like all we did was battle, and I feared it would be a battle to the death.

On the morning of 11 February, even though it was a Saturday, I woke up at my usual time of 6 a.m. I turned on my phone and there was a video from Brianna that she'd sent me the previous night, long after she had stormed upstairs and disappeared into her room, long after I had gone to bed, switched off my phone and gone to sleep. We kept quite different hours. I have been going to bed early and waking up early since the children were tiny.

I watched the video she had sent and couldn't stop myself from crying. A young trans woman had taken her own life, having waited several months for gender-affirming

7

care. I felt absolutely heartbroken for her and her family, and so much in that short video was terrifyingly familiar to me. I cried, just imagining what they were going through.

My God, I thought, to lose a child. It was my greatest fear. I typed back.

That poor family.

Brianna and I communicated best by text – in-person conversations drew too much heat. The day before, there had been a lot of tense back and forth between us about the shortage of the nasal spray she took to suppress testosterone. She was frustrated about having to wait a few months for it to arrive, even though we had gone private to get it, but all that melted away when I read her sweet text that morning.

*The NHS is so bad stuff like this makes me feel grateful
for a few months waiting with gender gp, that's so sad x*

Brianna didn't often voice her gratitude. Mostly, she demanded things, sometimes she broke things, frequently she shouted things and, on a few horrible occasions, she had thrown at me the ultimate threat: that she would take her own life. So to receive that gentle text of gratitude was huge for me because we had had such a horribly tough week. Who am I kidding? It had been a horribly tough few months.

The previous Tuesday, I had left work early to go with Brianna to a readmittance meeting at her school. Brianna had, once again, been suspended for refusing to adhere to school rules about uniform, being on her phone and back-chatting teachers. I'd just been given a promotion at work to the position I'd long aspired to do and it was my first full week in the role. Finally, I'd been made senior food technologist, and I was over the moon, so it is fair to say I was not best pleased about having to leave work to go into school, again. I was even less pleased about what happened when I got there. At the meeting, Brianna just sat there, focusing only on her phone, refusing to participate. When I asked her to put the phone down, she was so rude to me that the teacher intervened on my behalf and told her to stop speaking to me like that. As a result, her suspension was not lifted. She returned home to her bedroom to live through her bloody phone, unsupervised and unchecked, because since turning sixteen she kept her passcode from me and refused to give me access to what she was doing online. I returned to work and for the next two days threw myself into my new role. Thank God for work: at least I felt I was doing a good job at something.

I knew taking on more responsibility at work was going to add to the stress I was feeling about Brianna's deteriorating behaviour, but private hormone treatment does not come cheap and the extra money would help. I was also very concerned about the toll everything was taking on my other daughter, Alisha, and my partner, Wes. We were deeply worried about the educational path Brianna was on, and the fear she may be permanently excluded from school and would never make it to college was all-consuming. On top of that, I was increasingly nervous about who she was talking to online. Of all the things I worried about – and there were many – my greatest fear was that she would naïvely give out our address to people who might not be who they appeared to be. With Wes and me out at work, a recurring image haunted my thoughts: that one day I would come home and something terrible would have happened to Alisha and Brianna. It was this fear that had driven me to compile a letter back in January to Brianna's social worker effectively begging for help:

I am worried that she may be handing out our address,
I worry that I'll come home from work one day to find
both my children raped and murdered.

That thought made me feel sick, and I had been feeling sick all the time. I am fully aware that I am an anxious person, and I had learned the hard way, years before, what I needed to do to take care of my own mental health and untie the knot of fear in my gut. To counter the stress, I had taken up German and piano lessons – nothing like vocabulary tests and the D minor scale to focus the mind. At that time I worked four days a week, so on Friday, even though she was only upstairs, I texted Brianna to remind her that I was popping over the road for my piano lesson but would be back to meet the social worker who was coming at 1 p.m. After months and months of my frustrated calls, increasingly irate emails and desperate letters, the social worker was finally coming to the house to meet with Brianna so I needed her up and ready. I had already given the woman a comprehensive detailed description of the battles we were up against so when she arrived I didn't hold her up and, after a brief conversation with me, she went to speak to Brianna on her own. Brianna did not want me anywhere near her so I don't know what they discussed. On her way out, the social worker took me to one side and said something had come up about which she would speak to me later.

Left with only my imagination to chew on as to what that might be, I got food ready for our Friday evening meal – which Brianna would not join us for, or indeed eat. Alisha came home from college – she was in her final year of A-Levels and was working hard, and Wes got in from work. We were all tired and just wanted a quiet night at home in front of the telly. I cannot remember, genuinely, how the argument between Brianna and me started, but my guess would be it was about not going to school and generally refusing to get off her phone. Ever. Wes – my laid-back, patient, supportive partner – finally lost his patience. I think Brianna called me the C word. Like the teachers, he tried to put his foot down and, completely out of character for him, shouted at her. 'Do not speak to your mum like that! She is trying to help you.' I knew then we had reached breaking point. Wes never shouts.

Brianna stormed upstairs and locked herself in her room. We didn't see her again that evening.

So now you see why I was so taken aback by Brianna's thoughtful message on that Saturday morning. Maybe we were turning a corner? During the rest of the morning there was a flurry of texts that gave me cause to hope and I clung to them.

B: *Are you going to give me pocket money this Sunday?*
Me: *I'll start giving you pocket money when you're back in school and behaving yourself.*
B: *Email school and ask if I can come in on Monday.*
Me: *I'll be in work, but I will do.*

Alisha and I left the house around 10 a.m. It was a bright but overcast day and we drove to Planet Ice to get our ice skates sharpened. Anything that required real concentration was a way to practise mindfulness and take my mind off the bigger stresses. I was trying to build it into our lives. Coming out of lockdown, I thought we all needed a bit of extra self-care and fun. I know the positive power of gaining a skill. It's how I built my life back up from the ruins of my early twenties. Luckily, Alisha was a willing partner in crime. On our newly sharpened skates we headed out on to the ice to practise for our exam the next day. It was hard and hilarious in equal measure. I like to think we were getting quite good, good enough to pass the exam, anyway. On the way home we decided to go and see my mum for a cup of tea and a catch-up. It was at Mum's that I got another text from Brianna.

12.46 *I'm leaving to see Scarlet.*

It was even better than the gratitude text; she was getting out of the house, in daytime. I had been trying for months to get her to go outside, get some sunshine on her face. I was so pleased that I told Alisha.

'She's going to meet a friend.'

It was massive – she was going to go out with a real person.

The dogs are locked up.

OK, I replied. I couldn't appear delighted, as it would have pissed her off, but I was. I was delighted. Could this day get any better? At 1.41, it did.

1.41 *I'm on the bus by myself.*

Joy and relief flooded through me. I knew that Brianna wanted to be a 'normal' teenager more than anything, someone who was confident and sociable enough to do what her peers did – go out with friends, hang out at the shopping centre or just go to McDonald's. This was it, this was the first step. She was out. Maybe the combination of the news of that poor girl's death, the threat of permanent exclusion, the social worker's home visit, maybe even Wes getting cross and the teachers drawing a line, maybe the

13

knowledge that we were doing everything we could to support her was finally sinking in. We all wanted the old Brianna back, that giddy, cheeky, noisy child who messed about, took the piss, loved attention and always had a laugh. Another ping from my phone.

I'm scared.

She attached a photo of her feet on the bus.
I typed back.

That's well good.

I didn't want to acknowledge that she was scared, I wanted to keep the messages positive. More than anything, I wanted her to know that it was brilliant she had got on the bus, by herself, even though she was scared. It was huge progress. Face your fears, and the seemingly impossible becomes possible. Maybe the terrible phase of chronic isolation was coming to an end. She was meeting up with a real person, not anyone I had met, but I had heard about her. Now was not the moment to nag her about the inappropriately short skirt and the eye-catching long schoolgirl white socks, because, hey, pick your battles, right? I was too delighted she was out. I could leave the other battles for another day.

Why was getting on the bus so huge? Because my second biggest fear for Brianna, after who she was talking to online, was how on earth she was going to get to college, let alone cope with it. She was point-blank refusing to go to school but had shown some interest in studying hair and beauty at college – for this she certainly had a natural flair and talent, and a few weeks earlier she had been offered a place at Warrington and Vale Royal College. Trouble was, I had no idea how I was going to get her there. I had to leave the house by 7 a.m. to get to work so she was going to have to get a bus, and she had never, ever been on a bus by herself. I worried she wouldn't manage it and would retreat further and further online. I showed Mum and Alisha the photo.

'I can't believe it – she's on the bus!'

This is what I was thinking as I drank tea in my mum's living room. Brianna's going to be able to get to college. She's going to have a life. She's not spending the day speaking to strangers; I know who she's with; I feel she is safe. That was more than 'well good'. It was a miracle. I was so relieved. Saturday, 11 February was turning into a perfect day.

To read all her messages now, I have to scroll down to the bottom of my inbox because these days she doesn't text me back. That was the last message from me she could have read, but there are no blue ticks next to it, so I don't know if she knew how proud I was of her for getting on that damned bus.

Alisha and I got home around 3 p.m. Wes was back at the house playing on his PlayStation, so I joined him on the sofa for a bit, made some snacks for us both and was happy to chill. It was a precious, peaceful moment, the like of which had been sorely missing in recent months. Right on time, the dogs started getting impatient for their walk so I called Brianna to tell her we were taking them out. It went straight to answerphone. I didn't think anything of it; she was on her phone so much it regularly ran out of battery. There is a large landscaped wooded area surrounding the business park near our house; since we were feeling a bit sluggish and lazy, we decided to take the dogs for a quick walk there. We set off around the back of our house but when we got to the road leading to the business park, we saw more police cars than I had ever seen in one place. Something big had clearly happened.

'I wonder what's going on,' I said to Wes, and, being kind of nosy, we went through a few options: car chase, drug bust, someone famous? At some point I said, as a joke, that maybe Brianna had been caught shoplifting. I wish she *had* been caught shoplifting. We carried on walking towards the park, but there were so many police cars it was a bit intimidating, so rather than go past them we turned around and ended up walking home. It was a very short dog walk.

We were still talking about what could possibly have happened when we arrived at the flats that run along the back of our road. There was another police car parked right outside the block.

'If Brianna doesn't come home soon we may need to get the police back here . . .'

Then we turned the corner and I saw two things. Another police car, and our front door was open. Wes and I walked in through the small garden gate that I have now watched Brianna walk out of a million times on the final footage of her leaving home. There were two police officers standing just inside the threshold of our home. One was stocky, practically filling the door frame, but I could see Alisha behind him, at the bottom of the stairs, holding on to the banister. Alisha was safe, Alisha was safe, so this was something to do with . . .

'What's going on?' I asked.

'Do you want to come in?'

What sort of question is that? I remember thinking. It's my house; of course I want to come in. But I also remember thinking I really *didn't* want to go in. I think I knew something terrible lay on the other side of that threshold. *Breathe, Esther.* I stepped inside.

'You might want to sit down.'

'I don't.'

Now I definitely knew.

There was an awkward pause.

'Are you sure you don't want to sit—'

'Just tell me.'

There is life before this moment and there is life after this moment, and yet somehow I had already crossed this fracture in time, as in the dark crevasses of my soul I had known we were heading here, I just didn't know how or when or where.

'A body has been found.'

Now I knew when.

'I knew it,' I cried out. 'I knew this was going to happen. I knew it.' That's all I could say. It felt like it was all I had been saying, yelling, screaming, pleading, for months. Something terrible is going to happen.

It was her. I knew that.

'Her bank card was found near her,' one of the police officers told me. It's weird the things you think about when you are in shock. Why did Brianna have her bank card on her? She had no money in her account, as I'd withheld her pocket money until she went back to school. Maybe that's why she wanted to go back to school – she wanted to save up for a pink car. A job would be a better way, but she'd need qualifications for that, so she really had to knuckle down and finish school.

'Multiple wounds,' they said. 'Unclear if they were self-inflicted or if she was attacked.'

Self-inflicted? Attacked? What?

They didn't know what had happened. All they could tell us was that the person they believed to be Brianna had died at the scene. If it was her, she was dead. I knew it was her. They knew it was her. There was something about a liaison officer, an offer of tea and a promise that they would do everything . . . everything . . . to find out what had happened to her. The police took her PlayStation so they could trace who she'd been talking to and if she'd arranged to meet anyone. It is how paedophiles groom children online. The moment a child is online, they have access to the whole world. But worse, the world has access to *them*. Usually in disguise.

'I knew this would happen.' I kept saying it, or thinking it, or screaming it. I can't remember.

They told me from the beginning that speculation at this point was pointless and painful. They would collect the facts. So I told them the only fact I knew: that she had got on the bus and gone to meet her friend. I only knew the first name, so that was all I could give them. Of course, kids tell their parents all sorts of things; just because that's what Brianna had told me, didn't mean it was true. Sadly, in this case, it was.

By the end of that day, they had her friend's full name, but the couple who had found Brianna and who had made the 999 call had seen two people on the disused railway path that ran through a wooded area called Culcheath Linear Park. A girl and a boy. The boy looked like he was bending down to pat a dog, or put a lead on what they thought was a dog, while the girl looked straight at them before the two of them disappeared through the hedgerow and started jogging across an adjacent field. They thought the boy and girl had left a life-sized doll, so vividly white did she look, but as they got closer they realized it was a person and that person was in real trouble. Cheshire Police put out a press release asking for witnesses. The calls came in thick and fast.

19

Dash-cam footage too. Many people had noticed the girl in the thick white fluffy hoody, the inappropriately short skirt and the eye-catching long socks. I'd hated the fights we had about how short her skirt was. We had vicious battles about it. I begged and pleaded and sometimes I got mean.

She was walking up the stairs ahead of me.

'Your arse is hanging out, Bree!'

'You're jealous because you haven't got a bum like mine.'

'Please, just cover up a little bit, just to be safe.'

'You're such a middle-aged freak.'

The fights were constant, endless and exhausting, but looking back I am absolutely relieved that I lost every single one. I have been trolled on countless occasions by people who tell me what a terrible mother I am for letting my child go out dressed like some anime porn character, but now I say, well done, Brianna, well done for being yourself and dressing the way you wanted to. You were so unforgettable that 120 witnesses recalled seeing you and phoned the police. After all those times of giving her hell about what she was wearing, now I was glad she didn't blend in the way I wanted her to blend in, because with the help of each of those 120 calls, the agony of not knowing what had happened was over within days. Being eye-catching meant your killers got caught.

'You will have to come in for a formal identification.' That's when I broke. I remember my head hitting the table and the tears erupting. No. No. I couldn't do that. Surely there was another way. Wes said he would go, but I couldn't ask him to do that. The police left soon after and suddenly it was just the three of us. The house felt freakishly empty. The pain wrapped its vice-like grip around me and squeezed. My child was dead and my other child was terrified a murderer who might know where we lived was on the loose and could kill us all. Alisha and I stuck to one another like glue while Wes went and got the strongest tablets he could buy. We took them just to help us sleep. The three of us lay in bed and listened to an audiobook, anything to drown out the horror playing out in our heads.

I knew from previous experience that I could not let my dark thoughts take me down. I had to stay strong for my terrified, traumatized child. I had to stay strong for both of them. Eventually Alisha and I fell asleep. Wes waited until we were breathing evenly, then he went downstairs, checked all the locks and waited for morning. Until 3.13 p.m., Saturday, 11 February had been a near-perfect day, but from the moment my eyes opened the following morning I knew from the aching hole in my heart and indeed in the house that there would never be a perfect day again. Our future had been annihilated. Our past, too. I would not let myself think about Brianna's last minutes, but her last hours, days, weeks and months became something of an obsession for me. Yes, someone had killed my child, but something else had been killing my child for a while beforehand.

They say pick your battles. Well, this battle picked me.

2

The Ducks Are Screaming

Nature has played a big part in my life because, for the most part, nature is free. I am the only child of a single parent who, juggling several jobs, managed to put a roof over my head and food on the table and, even though our house was a jumble of second-hand furniture, my mum made it lovely. When I finally got my shit together and moved my own two tiny children into a place of our own, the childhood I replicated was, I realize, my own. Mum used to do her ironing in the living room while we watched our favourite programme, *Wizadora*, with the gas fire on, feeling cosy, relaxed and safe. For me and the kids it was CBeebies, *64 Zoo Lane* and *In the Night Garden*. Though I wasn't ironing in the background, I was curled up on the sofa, the jam in a kid sandwich. I know now that *Wizadora* was designed to be an English-language teaching tool, so I think Mum was drip-feeding education into my system from a young age, as she was always strict about what I could watch (*The Simpsons* was definitely banned as not age appropriate!) although she was very laissez-faire in other ways. Mum was far less strict when it came to looking after her grandchildren. They would often 'run away' to Grandma's to get thoroughly spoiled – right up to the bitter end, Brianna was threatening to run away to Grandma's. My sole goal now is to be there for Alisha if she has children. I will spoil them, but more than anything, I would like to make the world safe for them. Or at the very least, safer. It is a huge reason why I get out of bed in the morning. It is a driving force that makes me go on. Brianna is the one with her foot to the pedal, steering me on. The energy of my child was boundless, and it still is.

Mum left school at sixteen and didn't go back to college until she was in her thirties, eventually qualifying as a maths teacher and getting a job at the school I would go on to attend. For the record, having your mum work at the school where you are trying to sneak off for cheeky fags is not ideal. But we will get to that. For now, we live at Flaxely Close and she and I are truly peas in a pod. Mum didn't drive back then so we would walk everywhere. According to Mum, this took quite a long time because I was a very jolly child who liked to chat to everyone. What she remembers most about our walks was everyone saying hello. To me.

'Hello, Esther. Hello, Esther,' was the soundtrack of our walks. Later, when Mum had passed her driving test and earned enough to buy her precious little white Metro, the soundtrack changed. She would pick me up from primary school and we would drive further afield on bigger adventures than the back garden. I was always so excited to see that little white car. She used to listen to the music of her youth – Hall and Oates, Nirvana, INXS – and we'd drive along laughing our head-banging heads off. I still listen to that music, and now, Alisha does too. It's our comfort music, and thinking about it makes me cry. It is surprising what makes me cry these days.

'You can call him Dad, you know. He's your dad too.' My half-sister stated this fact once when I was visiting my other family on one of my annual trips to Cornwall. Once a year, Mum insisted on driving me all the way to Cornwall to drop me with the man who was my biological father but who I only ever called Pete. Then she would drive all the way home again to Warrington. Two weeks later she would repeat that monster drive to pick me up and take me home. I have very fond memories of my trips to Cornwall, mostly involving food. Pete and I would go crabbing and then cook and eat our freshly caught crabs. We would collect duck eggs for breakfast and dig for potatoes in the vegetable patch at the top of their steeply tiered garden. He tried to teach me to surf, but I wasn't a natural. I loved his dog, Gellert, but I also remember missing Mum and finding it hard to adjust to the salty smell, sleeping in a strange bed and trying to slip into a family dynamic that was and yet was not mine. In Cornwall I had a grandmother, Granny Ruth, who lived in a huge bungalow with what I remember as a massive garden, where she fed me chocolate Hobnobs with cups of tea to the ticking of a very large grandfather clock. Pete's partner had a little bug car and she would drive us to a park where they had boat swings. And once, when she took me for a walk along the estuary, I saw sprats swimming in one of the inlets. When I was a bit older there were family trips to the pub, ominously called the Bucket of Blood, for which Pete had made some of the furniture and where I pestered my half-sister to buy me some mead. I'd heard it was made of honey, so I was a bit disappointed when I got a mouthful of very strong alcohol.

Over the years, I had a fun time in Cornwall with my half-siblings, I loved the beach, and I got on very well with all of them, but I never called Pete Dad and I got all the love I needed from Mum at home. As I got older I was discovering there were other things to play with than boat swings and sprats, and the trips were expensive, so by the time I was eleven I stopped going.

Back when I was little, I spent a lot of time by myself outside and could make games out of the strangest things. There was a strip of cobbles as you drove into the cul-de-sac where our house was. It was a safety strip so cars slowed down which meant kids could play safely outside. In the heat, the tarmac that held them in place would bubble up and I'd spend happy hours sitting on those cobbles waiting for those bubbles and then squishing them back into place. An early game of Space Invaders, if you like, but very, very analogue. Even in the rain I would run about outside, dressed in nothing but knickers, until I was so filthy I could leave a slippery trail of mud on the slide. I would 'help' Mum cook – she was always a great provider of food – by stirring pots twice my size, but mostly I was an outdoorsy kind of kid and probably a bit of a tomboy. My grandad was still cycling to the gym when he was in his eighties and would cycle to Wales and go wild camping, so I think my love of nature is in the blood. Alongside an innate need to get away and regroup.

It wasn't all being Mum's little helper and playing make-believe, I also had a naughty streak and was just as likely to do what I was told – like Alisha – as I was to do the opposite, like . . . yes, you guessed it. When I was about six I had two pet mice. They lived in a cage in the shed by the side of the house. One day my mum shouted at the top of her voice for me to come downstairs. Immediately! I thought, uh-oh, that was her angry voice and I was in trouble, and I went downstairs wracking my brain about what it was all about. But I wasn't in trouble – Mum was pointing excitedly at the cage. There was a mass of squiggly, tiny pink things in the cage. Our mice had had ten babies. They became very cute quite quickly, growing fur and running around the cage in the shed. My mum's instructions were very clear.

'Do not, under any circumstances, put your hand in the cage, Esther.'

One day I snuck outside to do just that. I lifted the lid

off to reach inside and before I had time to even stroke one of the baby mice they had all jumped out of the cage and escaped. Not one was left. A lesson learned? Listen to your mother: she may know what she is talking about? 'Fraid not. It took more than a litter of missing mouse pups for me to listen to my mother and many years later, the mice long forgotten, my kids wouldn't listen to me either. I vividly remember telling them not to open the tank of the corn snake. One morning the snake was gone. Turns out 'somebody' had lifted the lid. Alisha swears even now it was not her. Brianna is no longer here to confirm or deny, but I have my suspicions.

I went to Gorse Covert Primary School and became friends with a girl who lived around the corner from me, and we would play out together sometimes and go to each other's houses. She had a nice big house and a collection of cupcake dolls. I must remember them because I coveted them, though I don't recall being jealous. I do remember her dog Tilly, whose entire backside would wiggle when I came through their back garden gate. At primary school I was sometimes picked on. I was quite an insular child, probably a bit odd, and a bit overweight. When I was seven an elephant at Chester Zoo gave birth and the baby elephant was named Esther. I remember seeing it on the evening news and my heart sinking. School the next day would be a minefield of jokes heading my way.

Needless to say, I preferred adults. I wasn't quite so sure about children. To cope in primary school I developed a bit of a facade: the cheeky, smiley kid, up for a laugh, up for anything that would mean no one picked on me, but Esther the Elephant was going to be hard to smile through. I wish putting on an act wasn't necessary, but we all know kids can be right little blighters and often mean. Sometimes seriously mean. I believe now that it's all just a coping strategy, but some coping strategies are better than others. I was lucky because when I had difficult days at school I could walk home and leave them at school. For Brianna, it was the opposite. At school she was relatively safe, but the real bullies were in her pocket. They would follow her into her room and into her head. If I had known what she was reading and seeing online, maybe I would have been able to counter it. But I didn't know, so I couldn't help. My mum would do something nice if I needed cheering up: my favourite, unsurprisingly linked to food, was the home-made box of chocolates. Milk Trays were over our budget, so she would buy a Mars bar and a Snickers bar, carefully chop them into squares and place them into a long-emptied box of chocolates. We would play at picking out our favourites and my worries would melt away. She was clever like that.

Sometimes when I got sick of being called Mrs Blobby I would deflect the attention using a rather less palatable strategy. Katy, my friend from over the road, seemed to struggle with her emotions and would occasionally burst into tears in class. This made her a target. She was below me in the pecking order of our form and I vividly remember choosing these moments to be mean to her. I am ashamed to say it happened a number of times. Probably because I got a good reaction, I played to the crowd, even though I never felt proud about it afterwards. The little flash of power was quickly replaced by an uncomfortable feeling I chose to ignore. When we left primary school, I found out that her older brother, who I knew from going to her house, had been seriously poorly all that time and had since died.

Even though we lost touch when I moved to a different secondary school, my behaviour towards her always bothered me. Eventually I decided to reach out to her so that I could apologize for what I had done. She taught me a vital lesson. I asked for her forgiveness and in receiving it was able to lessen the grip of self-loathing I had on myself. Later in my life, when my children's stepmother, Laura, reached out to me to offer her heartfelt apology for any pain she might have contributed to in the past, I knew exactly what to do. Katy and I parted as friends. Laura and I became friends. I learned early on the power of forgiveness and that enemies often have more in common than they could possibly imagine. The difficult bit is getting out of the way of yourself, putting aside pride and ego, and taking that first important step to find out. Make the call. Write the letter. Send the email. Reach out the hand. Meet.

I'm extremely grateful to my childhood friend Katy for teaching me that invaluable lesson. I would like her to know that I rely on it every day.

I was only aware that my mum worried about money because she told me, not because I thought we lacked anything, since as far as I was concerned, we did not. But I became aware of the stress it put Mum under. Despite holding down three jobs, her salary was never quite enough, and with a mortgage to pay off, budgeting for the monthly bills was nail-biting. I remember having a dream that she was ripping her own ears off she was so stressed. A conversation in passing with a friend led to a decision Mum took which eventually led to her becoming a foster parent. As ever, these things happen in increments. This friend had a teenage daughter who wanted to come and live with him, but he only had a one-room place. We were nearby, so Mum suggested he rent a room off her. That was so successful that when the girl left, Mum answered an advert for a student pharmacist who was looking for lodgings near her work in the shopping centre. She was lovely, and a nice addition to our house. When she left, a friend of hers took the room. By the time Mum saw an ad in the paper for anyone interested in offering respite care to teenage girls, she decided that since it had gone so well with the three lodgers, it was something she could do. The money meant she could stop work and go back to college and get her teacher training. I went to school and Mum went to uni and the respite girls came and went.

'So,' said the leader of the teacher-training course, 'when you wake up at 3 a.m. to do your emails . . .' Mum laughed, but by the time she became a fully qualified teacher and was offered a position as Head of Maths, she learned he had not been joking. Once Mum was qualified, she had a steady salary which could be augmented by fostering. We left the house with the cobbles at the end of the road and moved to a larger one. More rooms meant Mum could offer respite care to whole families and, in due course, groups of siblings. The first to arrive was a family of five, and they were great. I don't know why they needed to be at ours, but I understood they needed a break and I understood we were the lucky ones, and I understood that even if you don't have very much, you have more than many. I also learned that grown-ups can go to school, do homework and sit tests. Which made better sense to me, because as I moved through primary school, although I was happy, I wasn't entirely sure school was a place where children should go. Well, not this child, who was always a bit too boisterous, a bit too chatty and a bit too ready to work the crowd for laughs. I was amazed when Alisha went to Gorse Covert Primary School herself that I had a child who did sit still, who committed herself to whatever task was put in front of her, who worked hard and got on with no trouble at school; less so than when I was presented with the opposite in Brett. I always said to the teachers when I was faced with another 'demerit', 'warning', 'detention' or whatever new cross was being placed next to Brett's name that I was grateful Alisha had come first. If it had been the other way round, I wouldn't have been able to get her a place anywhere. Though I don't remember being light-fingered at preschool. I don't remember coming home with pockets full of coloured linking number cubes that did not belong to me. I would like to think perhaps Brett was particularly interested in maths, but I am afraid he was more of a magpie than a mathematician.

There is something circular about looking back at my childhood, because the streets I walked as a youngster are the streets I later walked with my young ones. Energetic, cute children, all three of us. In the summer there would be a paddling pool out the front of my mum's house for her grandchildren, just as she'd once put a paddling pool out for me, a continuum of little ears tuned to the call of the ice-cream van or the 'ice-cream-man van', as Brett would call it. Special places like Formby and Crosby beach, which my mum took me to when she had learned to drive and saved enough for a car, were the beaches I took my kids to when I learned to drive and saved enough for my own car after getting a job as a cleaner at a local car dealership. For me, uni came later. Mum and I were both single working mothers who eked out money to spare for visits to National Trust places like Speke Hall and Tatton Park.

Going full circle, my mum would take her grandchildren to play at the Haven kids' club, Brett's absolute favourite. What wouldn't I give to go back to those everyday moments. Buttering toast for breakfast, walking them to nursery with Brett in the pram and Alisha standing on the buggy board between my arms. I would drop them at nursery then get on the bus to the gym, and after that I would go home and clean the house so that it was always spotless. By this time, there had been enough mess in my life and I wanted to make amends to my wonderful, bonny, boisterous children.

The very best of childhood was for my children as it was for me, and in writing this book I realize I was walking in my mother's footprints for longer than I knew. The only difference was that she had one child and I had two, and even though she often helped me out with the kids, as they grew older and Brett became more and more boisterous, sometimes two was too much for her. Who am I kidding? Sometimes two was too much for *me*, so we would regularly divide and conquer, which allowed me to have precious time with each of my children separately. Alisha was a breeze of a child, a bit bossy, but easy to parent. With Brett, from the moment he could walk, I needed eyes in the back of my head. He was incredibly sweet, don't get me wrong, but was fast growing into a mischievous ball of energy that was new to me. He was that kid who always managed to find the biggest stick and wield it about dangerously, he was the kid who when faced with a sign that said Do Not Touch just couldn't help himself. Every puddle, every hazard, every accident waiting to happen, that was Brett. That is why this next memory is embedded in my mind. We were sitting side by side on a wooden jetty, as still and quiet as the waters of Lymm Dam; he seemed as awed by our surroundings as I was. After a while a family of ducks glided by and, quacking loudly, broke the silence.

'And the ducks screamed,' shouted Brett, leaping up, gleefully joining in. The ducks flapped furiously and flew away. It was just like when he saw his friends. He could never contain his excitement and it could be a little over-whelming. 'Where did the ducks go?'

I didn't have the heart to tell him that he'd scared them off.

Eventually the social worker in charge of respite care asked Mum if she would consider taking foster children in full time. It was a big decision, and it was one I was included in from the start. As I got older, Mum would insist I came into the meetings with the social workers, as it was my home too. They allowed this sometimes, but sometimes there were things my young ears were not allowed to hear. Mum used to get a bit pissed off about this, but I wonder now whether, because I had been sitting alongside her in the passenger seat of her life, it was easy to forget I was a kid too. The sisters came first, and they needed a lot of time and care. Mum took care of them, and we all walked to school together. I think Mum felt like Mary Poppins at times, with her ducklings trailing obediently behind her. I can remember quite clearly my own Mary Poppins moments, plaiting Alisha's beautiful red hair and looking down at her as I walked her to school and being bowled over by love and pride and joy and gratitude. I don't think there is a word big enough to encompass all that a mother can feel for a child.

The two sisters were at primary school when we were joined by two brothers, who were three and eight. Now there were five of us kids in the house. It was really nice and, even though there were constant scuffles and fights, I have fond memories of that time. I enjoyed having 'baby' brothers and sisters. Mostly. But I saw for myself that it isn't easy taking in confused, displaced children and making them feel safe and, as I would later learn myself, trauma travels on the inside.

'We're going to have chips, sausage and beans,' said Mum on the first day the boys came to us. 'Everyone sit down.' One of the boys burst into tears and ran to the stairs, where he collapsed into a weeping heap. Mum went to console him. If he didn't like chips or beans or sausages, it was fine; we could eat something else. He liked beans, he said. That wasn't the problem, but he wanted the whole can of beans to himself. He didn't want to share. It took Mum a while to understand that at home he would have been given a whole can of beans to eat from cold and he was upset because he thought he was going to have to share his can. Having children permanently placed felt different from respite care and gave me a new understanding that some kids really do have a horribly tough start in life. I knew we didn't have a lot, but it was a lot more than them. Mum was always open with me about who was coming to live with us and why, and nine times out of ten, drugs were involved. The boys' parents were also both full-blown heroin addicts, in and out of jail, who would periodically get clean, reappear, relapse, cause havoc and each time disappear back into addiction and crime, which would destabilize the boys. Mum worked really hard to rectify the situation and tried to give to them everything she had given to me – foundations from which to grow – but as I would discover myself, children don't always grow according to plan.

As a bit of an introvert myself, I was happy to spend time at home with my youngest foster brother. I spent hours building him a car out of cardboard boxes. Outside the house, it was a bit different. The thing was, he, like me, was an overweight kid with a great, big, round face. By then I was a deeply self-conscious sixteen-year-old so the idea of being seen out with him was mortifying. I had been picked on enough. Away from home I tried to distance myself from him as much as possible. Obviously, I know how that sounds, but he was more than capable of getting his own back. Once he picked up the dog poo and threw it at me. But mostly, I recall having fun. Mum and I were a team, and I think that meant we were caring for them together, providing a safe place, rather than her being the sole carer. We were all kids, but there were differences. I had been raised in a calm, quiet, safe environment from the beginning, with a loving mum and grandparents who adored me. I was shown a love of nature, I was taught gratitude and shown the resilience of others less fortunate than myself. I knew I was Mum's world, so I believe it was fair of her to assume that, of the five of us, the one least likely to fall into the hellhole of drug addiction, after all the damage I knew it caused, was me. I am so unbearably sorry, Mum.

3

You Have to be Smart to
Become a Doctor

I was eleven years old when Mum took in one particular foster kid to stay at ours for respite. Sometimes respite care is so the kids can have a break from parents who are struggling with addiction or their own mental health problems, and sometimes it is the other way around. I know now that this kid would come into the house in the evening having taken Ecstasy. But I didn't recognize gurning at the time and just thought he looked odd. A girl who lived with us at that point was around the same age as him – about fourteen at the time – and I used to spend a lot of time sitting in her room, chatting and listening to music. He must have fancied her because he kept coming in and trying to chat her up, but it was confusing because it wasn't pleasant.

'You think you're something, don't you . . . flaunting yourself . . . not that fit . . . though I wouldn't kick you out of bed . . .' And the age-old derogatory compliment: 'Nice tits.' It was unpleasant to hear and see, but he had quite a forceful personality and he took up a lot of space. Looking back now, I can see that witnessing that was unsettling and I think I was probably a bit afraid of him but trying hard to look cool. From then on, I spent a lot of time trying to look cool and appear older than I was. It was this boy who brought aerosol cans into my home. In the bathroom he taught me how to 'toot' – a skill I was determined to perfect. After he left, I graduated to buying cans of air-freshener and inhaling chemicals with my mates until I passed out. I'm not saying it was all his fault me becoming interested in getting wasted, but the influence he had on me was real. I think about that word – 'influence' – a lot these days. He was just one boy who altered the trajectory of my life. Whereas Brianna was 'influenced' by an unrelenting, constant barrage. What happened to me is far from the worst story I've heard about being brought up in a home full of foster children, and mostly I am glad Mum did it, but there was a darker side. It wasn't all Mary Poppins and plaited hair. Sadly, childhood can end prematurely and abruptly, and it makes adolescence and finding your young feet in an adult world all the harder. I was eleven when I was introduced to drugs and alcohol. Brett was eleven when he got his first phone. The deterioration in our behaviour was different, but equally as fast and deep.

At Gorse Covert Primary School I had a few friends and a system by which I'd learned to survive. Play the clown. Get the laughs. Be the cheeky one and hide my growing insecurity about my appearance. But I still managed to do well in school. My SAT results were high, so, although as nervous as the next kid, I felt confident that I could cope with secondary school. On paper there was no reason why I should fail. However, when I moved to Birchwood High School, the size, pace and expectations threw me. I was unprepared and overwhelmed. I missed the small classes, I missed my friends who'd gone to different high schools; the few friends I had made were spread around the catchment area.

The teachers didn't take to my cheeky charms. I wasn't sweet Esther who once upon a time had said hello to everyone, I was just the annoying kid who kept talking when I should be listening. After a promising start it seemed to begin going downhill quite fast. For Alisha, that same hurdle came and went without any drama. When Brett followed, I held my breath, but the stricter secondary school I had chosen for them seemed, at first, to be working. I got a lovely email from his form tutor telling me how well he was doing.

I have had some amazing feedback about Brett from his English, maths and drama teacher. All of his teachers have said how well he is doing recently in terms of his focus during lessons, how he is asking relevant questions and performing well in these subjects.

I cannot tell you how relieved I was, because, for me, going from the top of primary school with teachers who've watched you grow, to the bottom of secondary school where no one knows you had been terrifying. I was particularly wary of the older kids. Some could be unbelievably mean. I was also becoming painfully aware of my changing self and was still conscious about my size. In the library, twin girls from a few years above pointed at me and announced loudly to their group that I had a galaxy of spots on my face. Ha, ha, ha. I was mortified. I was not going to be the kid who was pointed at again, I was not going to be Mrs Blobby once more, so I decided there in that library that I would find another way to protect myself. If the cheeky-clown act wasn't going to work, I would mimic what I had seen at home. I knew how the tough kids talked and I knew the reaction it got. I would not be the one being pushed and shoved in the hallways, so I started to act up. I talked back to teachers to disguise the fact that I couldn't cope. I would do anything to hide my insecurity, but it really was all an act.

'Esther Ghey, you have to remove that nose piercing. It is against school rules.'

'No!'

I'm not sure who was more taken aback, me or the teacher, but the thing is that I wasn't supposed to remove it. It might have looked like defiance, but it was actually fear.

'If you don't, there will be consequences.'

'I can't take it out!' I pleaded, and then burst into tears. I was scared of the teacher but, in that instant, I was more worried about wasting Mum's money if it closed up. Maybe if I had explained, maybe if the teacher had asked why, things would have worked out differently, but instead I dug in – I mean, it was only a nose ring – and there were indeed consequences. I was sent to sit outside the head's office. It was the first of a series of detentions I was given from the get-go, all for stupid things, in my precocious eleven-year-old opinion, but the regularity with which I was getting into trouble meant I often found myself sitting in the 'exclusion unit'. This was basically a wooden desk with metal legs placed outside the head's office. I suspect part of the punishment was the humiliation of being in the corridor, on public display, but for someone trying to create a hard persona, that didn't work. Especially if it got you the attention you craved. After a few months at secondary school, Brett, too, started getting into trouble for stupid things, like jumping on sauce packets in the dining hall. He was made to pick up litter. An equally visual punishment. When you understand the feeling that any attention is better than no attention, you can perhaps understand why I started to feel very afraid that history was going to repeat itself.

I kept my nose ring, and Mum didn't get cross and, sadly, rather than falling in line, I was emboldened by the experience. The rules didn't apply to me. I could stand up to teachers and get away with it. At the time, I thought this was a good thing. But when I became the parent of a child at the same school who railed against rules I forgot all about my own indignation and found myself constantly nagging Brianna – and I mean *constantly* – about those damn nails. They were so long, and they were definitely not school regulation. Did she care? No, she did not. Like mother, like daughter . . . and yet I can't help thinking, if I'd been putting on a front, all bravado and attitude, cocky enough to talk back to teachers but not confident enough to put my hand up in class, was she? I will never know now.

I didn't stop at stupid, silly things and, eventually, I pushed it further. In a science class towards the end of Year 7, I took on another girl and, once again, I didn't back down – I have no idea what it was about – but I ended up punching her. We became friends after that, but yet again, I found myself in the 'exclusion unit' and now banned from the classroom, my reputation as a gobby little scally upheld. Placing me in the exclusion unit had sealed my fate at Birchwood High. I was given worksheets to fill out, but I didn't bother doing them; instead, I graffitied them, drawing pigs, mostly. With their French name underneath: *cochon*. I imagine I thought I was being incredibly witty, but actually I was the one getting the pronunciation wrong. Penis humour, does it ever get boring to kids at school? When I was allowed back in the classroom I would just talk over the teacher until I was sent out again. I know exactly how irate with frustration I must have made my teachers as they watched my behaviour slide and my marks tank, because years later I had to watch Brett do the same thing in Year 7. The detentions came thick and fast, always for stupid things, until there were just too many of them and another solution had to be found. For us both, it meant transferring to another school.

I am constantly tripped up by the striking similarities between how my education played out and how Brianna's did, twenty-five years later. Why couldn't I see it at the time? My child was in the same exclusion unit I had been put in, but by then Birchwood High School was of course a different place. The exclusion room is no longer a desk outside the head's office, it is a separate space where children with special educational needs or who are struggling with anxiety or poor mental health, or who need to work off-syllabus can work quietly or catch up with a specially trained teacher, so that no one – hopefully – gets left behind. The head of my old school is a groundbreaking woman called Emma Mills who I now count as one of my greatest friends and strongest allies and who works at the sharpest end of the digital revolution. Brianna had every one of those needs and the school tried to accommodate them all, so for the few hours that she did go to school, it was to the exclusion unit that she went, and it too sealed her fate.

Back at the end of the last millennium, Mum concluded that I wasn't learning anything sitting outside the head's office at Birchwood High and managed to get me a place

45

at the school where she taught maths. How I would like to go back now and tell that child drawing pigs on her worksheets that bravado can only get you so far, and usually in the wrong direction. What would I not give to beg them both, Brianna and me, please, go back to your classrooms, you'll be safe there; get an education, build yourself a life. The lesson I should have learned at that point was that the person leading the class was trying to teach me something, if only I would listen. The lesson I should have learned was to have some respect for that person trying to teach me something. The lesson I should have learned was that I had a lot to learn, namely that I didn't know best and that I should care about my own chances in life, and that I was worth that investment, just as every child is. Instead, I left Birchwood, my bad habits came with me, and it would take several hard, painful years to finally learn those lessons. When Brett started playing up in Year 7, after that promising start, I stood shoulder to shoulder with his teacher, and that teacher tried very hard to get Brett to knuckle down and settle in. I took every knuckle rap and unsettling email extremely seriously and told Brett off for getting into trouble. I think now that I probably went too far the other way, and although I understand why, that hindsight haunts me.

Looking back, I don't think I should have left Birchwood. I think what I needed back then was a firm hand. I needed somebody to say, 'No, Esther, knuckle down. Don't get your nose pierced, don't break the rules; they are in place so every child can get an education. Don't distract the other kids, don't get into trouble and don't speak to teachers that way when they are trying to help you grow.' When I became a parent and saw Brett repeating my mistakes, I decided to do things differently. This is not about blame; it is about understanding that we are all the sum of our parts.

My mother is, at her core, naturally confident. I don't know if she gathered that confidence because she took care of herself from the age of sixteen, or if she was born that way. I do know that she wanted to get away from home as soon as possible and learn her life lessons on the road and was content to work and live hand to mouth until the time came when she had another mouth to feed. For those fourteen years, she'd travelled all over the place. She made and sold jewellery. She was a waitress. She worked in clubs. She juggled jobs and travelled to distant places; at one point she lived and worked on a kibbutz in Israel. She was adventurous. She was a free spirit who survived on her wits, and she had a great time doing it. I suspect she did exactly what she wanted, and when she wanted a baby, well, she made that happen too. It was only then that she needed qualifications, so she simply went back to school and got them. Now she was a maths teacher at the school I was on the verge of attending.

The overall message I got from all this was 'don't worry, you're a kid, be a kid. You can get to it all later.' I did get to it later but, unlike my mother, I did not have fun and adventures on the way. Instead I became a teenage mum and never left Warrington. Even if that hadn't happened, if I am being totally honest with myself, I am not sure I would have had the confidence to go off and do what she did. We are similar, but we are not the same. So, of course, I was terrified that Brett, who by the end of Year 7 was getting into trouble constantly, was going to saunter down the wrong road, just as I had. I thought my job was to build as many barriers as I could to stop that from happening. But it didn't matter what I tried, I failed miserably, and eventually the school and I agreed, just like with me at the same age, that he would be better off somewhere else. Somebody else's problem.

Sir Thomas Boteler School, where Mum taught, was further away from where we lived. It was smaller and less academic, which is maybe why they were happy to take a child with such good SATS results. Perhaps Mum kept quiet about the hours I'd spent at the exclusion unit table, because I was put in the class for bright kids, Form B, and they were absolutely lovely. The stick hadn't worked at Birchwood; maybe the carrot would work at Boteler. Although I may have appeared confident and cocky, inside I was still that insecure overweight kid, desperate to be picked rather than picked on. I hated PE for so many reasons, but the worst was having to wear dark blue shorts and a tight pale blue T-shirt. I hated showing my legs – still do – so it was excruciating having to sit outside the PE hall on a long wooden bench waiting to go in. A boy in my class pointed at me and made a comment about my shorts riding up and my thighs chafing. I must have looked like he'd slapped me.

'Don't worry,' he said quickly, changing his tone. 'Mine do too.' Perhaps he was trying to make me feel better, but it was too late: the damage was done. My thighs were big. My legs were horrid. I was mortified and embarrassed and ashamed all at the same time and wanted the world to swallow me whole. I think about these moments – the twins pointing out my spots in the library and the boy pointing at my thighs – I can remember them so acutely, and then I think about all the comments Brett got about being naughty and badly behaved, and the terrible comments Brianna got online, and all the bile I get now, and I wonder, if they could see my face, would they see the hurt and – like the boy in my class – try to take it back or make amends? Would they say, *Don't worry, mine do too*? I would like to think they would.

It is to my great shame that I quickly reverted to my primary-school coping strategy and rather than work to stay in Form B with those great kids, I worked hard at once more becoming the class clown. It was successful in one regard because, at last, I had friends, so now I liked going to school, but for the wrong reasons. School became a social event for me; lessons were just the backdrop to fun. I had a little crew; nothing new – skirt rolled up, a pair of precious Rockport boots on my feet, smoking fags behind the bike shed. It was a bit annoying that my mother taught at the school, so when she asked me whether she should take the head of maths role that she was being offered, or leave to become a full-time foster carer, I told her what a brilliant foster carer she was.

Without Mum at school, I had to take the bus. Two buses, actually, and I could taste freedom. I got confident in the wrong way fast and distinctly remember wandering into school, in no hurry, a bit cocky even though I knew I was late. Through the windows I could see my classmates already sitting at their desks. I would blame the bus and appear as nonchalant as possible. I don't think I am the first kid to cover up insecurity with false bravado and I know for a fact that I was not the last. I was sitting in a huddle of my mates in our science class when a new girl was introduced to our year. Louise still tells the story that as soon as I saw her, I shouted out to her and waved her over to join my merry gang of miscreants. I know I didn't feel that confident on the inside, but I must have been better at hiding it than I realized, because Louise assures me I seemed pretty sure of myself. I must have driven the teachers mad because I was still doing relatively well but with ever-diminishing effort, and as I moved up the school, it was going to catch up with me. I wasn't academic by any stretch of the imagination, but I didn't find lessons difficult either – except maths, which I was terrible at. In that regard, Brett and I were different.

He had profound dyslexia and terrible eyesight so for him secondary school was a loud, giant, out-of-focus maze and a jumble of incomprehensible instructions. I was just lazy and too busy trying to be cool. What I needed was a firm hand. What Brett needed was a gentle one. I don't think either of us got what we needed.

In my biology test at the end of Year 9, a subject I secretly loved, I got the highest score: 97 per cent. My biology teacher, Mr Atherton, who I also loved, tried in vain to encourage me to work harder and not waste my potential. But it fell on deaf ears. I kept mucking about, and then I got caught smoking. Another detention.

'What do you want to be, Esther?' asked my exasperated physics teacher, Mrs Waldron.

'I want to be a doctor,' I answered with my refined, veil-thin nonchalance.

'You have to be smart if you're going to become a doctor.'

I heard the put-down loud and clear. You are not smart enough to be a doctor. But I don't think that is what Mrs Waldron meant. I think she meant I had to be smart if I was going to become a doctor, and I was not being smart at the time. Certainly not smart enough to take my education seriously. Hearing that was perhaps the excuse I needed because, at that point, I gave up on myself. Eventually, the carrot was withdrawn and the stick returned. If I could not stop talking in class and distracting other students I would be sent out, I would fall behind, I would fail and I absolutely would not become a doctor. They didn't want me to fail, but I didn't stop and my teachers had no choice but to send me out. There was a little glass window in the door and I'd keep popping my head up and down, pulling faces to try to get my friends' attention. Years later, when I re-sat my biology GCSE, I found I still loved the subject; it was logical and interesting and I could do it. It is why I chose to do a science degree at university when I finally understood what all those teachers had tried to tell me . . . I like to think that Mrs Waldron's and Mr Atherton's attempts to get me to take myself seriously were not wasted, and I am thankful for that faith because, deep down, I never forgot it. It just took me a long time to hear it.

Louise and I became fast friends and she introduced me to the teenagers who lived on a run-down estate across the road from a park and a huge Homebase. From around the age of thirteen we would get older kids to buy us alcohol and we'd go to the park to drink. Sometimes we would all go into town and buy bags of air fresheners, then come back and toot so much of the stuff I would pass out. The less work I did, the more trouble I got into. And when I started drinking it got worse. It snowballed. Bad habits, bad crowd, bad behaviour, bad attitude, and all the time it looked like I was totally in charge. But I wasn't. I drank because I was nervous. I took drugs because I was drunk. I felt jittery and anxious in the days after a weekend bingeing, so I drank, so I took drugs, so I got more anxious, so I drank . . . and so it went on. Eventually the partying started to take its toll and I would feel strangely anxious walking into school. I made no link between drinking and tooting too much at the weekend, I simply concluded that I wasn't academic and school was not the right place for me. Mum soon agreed.

With little discussion, Mum and I decided that the best thing for me was to leave Sir Thomas Boteler and be 'homeschooled' – I'm not exactly sure by who? Mum? I can't recall that happening. I do know she just wanted me to find my own way to what I was good at and was happy that I would go into school for a few hours a week for the subjects that I enjoyed, Resistant Materials and Graphics. It is possible that the real reason why I agreed to those terms was because my great mate Louise would be doing them too. She and I were the only girls in a class of boys. Another big draw. Oh my God, we mucked about so much we reduced our teacher to tears. She could see what I could not. That I was flushing all my potential down the toilet and that it was going to end badly. She was right about that. My homeschooling involved playing the computer game *The Sims* all day and every day until I could head back out to the park to drink and toot to my heart's content. Every weekend we would head out to Mr Smith's nightclub to snog as many boys as we could. I was now sixteen and in a few short months I would be leaving school for good.

My life was just about to start, and I couldn't bloody wait. I now share my mum's deep-seated belief that no one's life should be decided by the tender age of sixteen. Hers wasn't. Mine wasn't. Brianna was not so fortunate.

4

Drowning

'You are not going out looking like that!' My mate Louise was tall and, more than anything, loved her shockingly short red dress with a boob-tube top. The perfect outfit for getting attention. Her dad would kick off quite a lot about this dress, just as years later I would nag Bree about that tiny, tiny skirt she loved to wear, but somehow, like Bree, Louise managed to get out of the house wearing it, and it was our secret weapon. Did I wear stuff like that? Not a chance. I would hide myself in black trousers and a black T-shirt, but it didn't matter: I had Louise and the boob-tube dress to do the work for me.

Don't you think you know everything at sixteen? Well, I certainly thought so. Maybe it was because it had just been me and my mum for so long, or maybe it was because I'd helped her look after the younger foster kids, or maybe it was just because I was a teenager. It takes a distinct lack of maturity to think you know it all, and I thought I did. We were not old enough to buy booze and fags but would still stand outside the shop and ask random people to go in and buy a three-litre cider bottle or big bottle of Lambrini and, pooling our pound coins of pocket money, always a pack of Richmond Superkings. Tanked up, we'd head to the out-skirts of town to Mr Smiths, the best night club in the area. Louise would always make me go to the DJ and ask for 'Rhythm of the Night', at which point we'd hit the dance floor and then see how many blokes we could snog. Louise usually beat me. Thinking back now, we hadn't a clue who these people were or how old they were. Anything could have happened, but we weren't thinking like that; we were invincible. Or at least I was pretending to be. We did at least, for the most part, stick together. I remember once a bouncer ran past me to break up a fight, sending me flying. I landed flat on my back on the dance floor; I was bruised for weeks. Lots of people were very friendly and helped me up, though, thinking back on it, maybe that friendliness was just the result of Ecstasy. There was a *lot* of Ecstasy about. To me, though, that was the sign of a good night out. I liked the place. I liked the scallies. More fool me.

Sometime in the spring, before we took our GCSEs, Louise met a bloke who was a few years older than us, and she started seeing him on and off. One night he asked us if we wanted to go back to his mate's house after the club. As soon as we got there, I knew I was out of place and out of my depth. Every room was rammed, there was a woman who looked so unwell I thought she might be on heroin, and people were openly sniffing coke. I'd never seen anything like it before and must have stood out like a sore thumb. An insecure schoolgirl in an oversized T-shirt, desperate for attention but trying to blend in; easy pickings, you could say.

Then as now it starts, as it often does, with a compliment.

'Ain't she got fit eyes, 'er.'

Reductive and derogatory, maybe, but powerful too, because the hook was instantaneous. These days they might not even bother with words:

It is my opinion that many young people are seeking validation of this sort and once they receive it, it is hard not to want more. Having never had a dad, I'd never witnessed a real relationship, functioning or non-functioning. Rather than be distrustful of the sudden bright light of attention, I was bedazzled, which is maybe why I was blinded to how messy things were from the start. Drinking sessions in the park bled into drinking sessions in the pub, which led to all-nighters in people's houses. There were frequent fights and arguments, people threw punches and insults so readily that I started thinking the relatively peaceful way of life I had known was the anomaly. Even with all the foster kids coming through our house, I had never seen anything like this.

Jealousy was usually the first spark, then drink and drugs would fuel the fights. I remember one night a woman smashed a metal ornament over her boyfriend's head. Off his head, he went zigzagging down the street, blood everywhere, then she got in her car and tried to run him over. Someone called an ambulance, but when it arrived he wouldn't get in because he was so off his face. The rest of us were panicking because there were drugs everywhere. It sounds awful now, but when I was sixteen, I thought all this madness and mayhem was fun. I was intoxicated by it, in more ways than one. I go cold thinking what would have happened if we'd had smartphones back then, phones with cameras. It wouldn't have taken long for the private humiliation to turn public. But like so many teenagers, I wasn't thinking about consequences. I didn't want safe, I didn't want boring, I wanted to be part of the action, and this was where I thought the action was. I was a foolish, foolish child, I admit, but I was only a child. I hadn't even left school. For the record, I bloody love boring now. And as for safe? What wouldn't I give for safe.

I know my mum didn't like what was happening.

'Will you stay in tonight?' Mum would ask me every now and then. 'Keep me company?'

I know now she was trying to save me from myself and the scallies I was hanging around with, but I was having none of it.

'Stop trying to control me. You're ruining my life.'

Sound familiar? Poor Mum. And what about my GCSEs? Well, who needed GCSEs? Not me, clearly. I left school that summer without a single qualification to my name. We will never know if Brianna would have followed my own ill-chosen path, but since she was going to be an 'influencer' and TikTok famous, she certainly didn't think GCSEs were important or necessary.

When my mum had left school at sixteen, her father made her wander the streets from 9 a.m. to 5 p.m. every day until she found a job. It was the middle of winter, so she found a job fast. Her equivalent dose of reality to me was to pay the deposit for a furnished flat. I think she hoped that when I found out what being a grown-up, independent person fully entailed I would change my mind and come back to the safety of home. Unfortunately, she underestimated my deepening lack of self-respect and growing insecurity. How could she see it, when she loved me wholly and totally, thought I was bright, capable and beautiful? It is very hard to understand when a person you love so much doesn't love themselves. Reality would soon bite, but not in the way Mum had hoped and imagined. Looking back now, over twenty years later, I would like to apologize to sixteen-year-old me, for thinking so little of myself. I would also like to apologize to my mum, for not listening to her.

It is my opinion that the use of drugs, social media and abusive relationships can mimic the highs and lows of each other. One minute you are high, on top of the world, put on a pedestal, adored; the next you are low, emotionally kicked to the ground, belittled and full of regrets. With all three, the pull to get back on a high is strong, even though the damage is clear. Is it love or is it MDMA? One minute you're blowing a whistle, in love with the world. The next you're stuck in a wardrobe in the foetal position, in such a mess that you can't get out. One minute you're everything. The next minute you're nothing. One minute you're celebrated. The next minute you're trolled.

You're ugly.

You're so fat.

Slag. No one would ever want you.
Don't you mean Brian?
Your son died because of you. You are a failure.

It is possible to pretend you don't care about the harsh words, but words can be weapons too. When I was trolled on Facebook after Brianna was killed, that particular comment struck me hard. *Your son died because of you. You are a failure.* It hurt precisely because I did feel like a failure. I was supposed to protect my child and I had failed. The comment was reported to Facebook by the police, but then, as now, I was told that the person causing the harm had a right to privacy, regardless of the hurt and damage that it caused me.

During those years between 2003 and 2004 I went back to my mum's house time and time again. But I would crave the validation and the attention, I would believe the excuses, and relapse instantly. It is my opinion that when someone says, 'sorry for any harm caused but it is only because I love you so much,' they are lying to themselves and to you. It is also my opinion that when someone says 'it will never happen again', after numerous times of already having done so, they are also lying. I believe I understand how kids feel these days, addicted to their phones, chasing the likes, needing a hit, wanting to feel that high again, but I also believe I understand the secrecy, the shame and the growing isolation. The definition of addiction is that you continue to participate in unhealthy actions even though you know they are bad for you. In other words, you can't stop, or you think you can't, or you are so afraid that if you do, you will be alone, but in fact, it is the thing you are addicted to that is keeping you from building meaningful relationships. I think I finally understand how similar Brianna and I were in that respect.

It is my opinion that if you think you are in an unhealthy relationship then you most likely *are*, and the longer you stay, the harder it is to get out. These days, methods of control are now so enmeshed in our digital world that a door camera can be used not just to keep people out but to keep a person in. It is well documented that historically abusive partners used to pull the phoneline out of the wall to keep other people away, but now they can monitor you 24/7, where you go, what you spend, who you text.

Mum had paid the deposit on the flat, but being young and irresponsible I was not very good at paying the bills, so before too long that was the end of the flat. So much for being an independent grown-up. I didn't have any friends. I didn't have a job. I didn't have any money. When I left Mum's yet again, it was to move into a shithole with no furniture except a single mattress with a broken spring. Getting pregnant was not ideal, but taking the pill would be considered to mean I must be sleeping around, so I couldn't do that either.

I desperately wanted to be a mum, even though I was only seventeen and broke. What else could I do? I didn't have any qualifications, I didn't have any aspirations, and what promise I had shown at school I had squandered. I thought the only thing that I could achieve was to get pregnant, have a child and try to be a good mum. In the end, it was the best decision I ever made, and when I found out I was pregnant I was overjoyed. I felt a certainty inside me that, no matter what I was dealing with, this was something I could do.

As soon as I got pregnant, I stopped taking drugs or drinking, which was good, but I started to gain a lot of weight, which was bad. My belief in myself – which was already quite low – began to nosedive.

'You fat cow!' the lads in the car yelled at me while I was crossing the road and then wound up their window and sped off. I wanted to stop that car, pull them all out, line them up in front of me and make them stop.

I know I'm fat. You think I don't know I'm fat? I'm told on a daily basis that I am a fat slag and no one would ever want me, let alone love me, I'm trying to do something about it, I'm walking to the gym, even though I am pregnant and tired, because everything is all my fault and I'm trying to change, I'm trying to fucking change!

I wish I had said that. I wish I had stood in front of that car and yelled from the top of my voice: YOU DON'T KNOW ME! YOU DON'T KNOW WHAT I AM GOING THROUGH. I'M JUST TRYING TO KEEP MYSELF FROM DROWNING!

I didn't. I hung my head, waddled to the gym, felt utterly shit about myself and played it back in my mind over and over. I can still see that car and those lads laughing at the one who had shouted; how clever, how funny, how impressive, what a brilliantly incisive observation. Every time I am trolled now, *you are a failure*, I find myself once again standing on that crossing. I want to put my hand through the phone screen and grab SpaceMonkey69 and shout, YOU DON'T KNOW ME! YOU DON'T KNOW WHAT I AM GOING THROUGH. But then I stop. I put the phone down. I am not the girl on the crossing any more. I could be hurt by a comment like that, or I could think about the person on the other side of the screen. I don't know them; I don't know what they are going through either. Perhaps we are all just trying to keep ourselves from drowning.

I was so utterly miserable at the time, that comment – *fat cow* – could have been the final straw, the thing that pushed me over the edge, and those boys in the car would never have known the devastating harm they would have caused. A flippant comment. A joke. It makes me incredibly sad that moments and comments like that are happening to teenagers every day. Bree said she didn't mind about the comments because she was getting likes too, but I wonder what it is doing to their brains now that it happens all the time. I can remember that moment like it was yesterday, but for young people now it is yesterday and today and every day before that and every day to come – unless we make it stop. I would really like to take everything I have learned since that moment on the crossing and help make it stop.

When Alisha was born, in January 2005, I suddenly understood what maternal love is and also how much I had been loved. For days and days, it was just me and her in a cocoon, but not for the right reasons. Yes, it was important we bonded with our new baby, but surely my mother could have been allowed to drive us home from the hospital? Mum was desperate to see me and meet Alisha. Left alone at eighteen with a newborn, I poured every ounce of love I had into Alisha. I may not have had the courage to stand up for myself, but when it came to my child, I would put her interests ahead of anyone's. I kept breastfeeding her despite feeling pressure to stop. Very occasionally, I would go out with Alisha to meet my mum but spent my precious time with her checking my watch, telling her I had to get back, just in case. It is my opinion that sometimes when people check in on you, they are really checking up on you. Mum says it was painful to watch, but she would always, always welcome me home. Sadly each time she then had no option but to let me go again. I want to shout back through time: *don't go, don't go! Don't go, Esther. Don't go, Bree. Please, don't go.*

I don't know if I have always been anxious or if it was becoming a mum so young, with all that responsibility for this little life, that made me anxious, but either way, I was and am a nervous mother. It drives Alisha mad that I grab for her hand when we are crossing the road. Actually, now, she lets me hold on a bit longer and a bit tighter. Walking Alisha when she was little became an ordeal for me. Just seeing that pram going first, out on to the road, with someone else pushing it, was enough to make my heart stop and, like now, I would reach out to protect her. It is my opinion that the small things do the most damage.

I showed Alisha a picture of me and her from that time and I am enormous; I look middle-aged, but I was only eighteen years old. I had made a lot of mistakes since turning sixteen, but having Alisha was not one of them. Looking at that photo now, I think the way I looked on the outside was a reflection of how I felt on the inside. Heavy, sad and not worth taking care of. I put all my love and energy into Alisha, but I didn't know how to take care of myself. I wish I had gone out with my mum and my new baby more. To the park, the library, maybe a toddler music group. But I didn't feel able to do any of that. I was increasingly alone. It was me and Alisha, but I realize now it was really just Alisha, because even while my weight was ballooning, I was disappearing.

I was terrified about having another child. Once upon a time it had been me and Mum, two peas in a pod; now it was me and Alisha. I knew that what strength I had went to her; there wasn't any more. I can't even remember being pregnant the second time, but I can remember giving birth. I was only in labour for about two or three hours and most of it was spent alone, worrying about Alisha and wanting my mum. This is how my beautiful baby boy came into the world, on 7 November 2006. Now with two small children to care for, my isolation was complete. I can't remember taking my newborn baby home to meet Alisha, but I do vividly remember the day in December when I called my mum sobbing from a phone box. This time, I knew, I was never going back. I may have been a broken twenty-year-old girl, but I was determined to break the cycle. I wanted my children to grow up in the same safe, loving – boring – environment that I had. Alisha was not even two and Brett was only three months old. Perhaps now it is easier to understand why years later that comment on Facebook hurt me so much. Even though I left, I failed to keep them safe. I still have that thought in my head: that it is all my fault. These days, thanks to all I have learnt from the mindfulness training, I notice that thought, I acknowledge it as a damaging echo of my past, and I let it go. Well, I try really hard to let it go.

5

Mum, You've Got Freckles!

The three of us stayed with my mum until I thought I was strong enough to cope with two children on my own. It started off so hopefully in the narrow three-bedroomed house we moved to, and I threw myself into making it as nice as I possibly could. I chose a teal-colour paint for the downstairs and bright pink for the toilet. I cut up self-adhesive tiles so they would fit on the floor, trying to make the house as lovely as my mum had always managed to make ours when I was little – our own home sweet home. If I had surveyed myself I would have said: Esther, a lick of paint isn't going to be enough to fix the structural damage underneath; you've been through a lot, you need help.

I was only twenty, had two children under two; I had been spat at, kicked at, I had lost every photo of Alisha as a baby and most of my belongings; I had lost touch with my real friends, had no qualifications and had very sadly come to believe that I was worthless, useless and unlovable. I wish I had got some professional help so I could have understood what I had been through. Instead I internalized all those painful experiences and turned the shame and self-loathing on myself. I felt broken, but hoped with enough paint the cracks wouldn't show. I am sorry to say, my life was going to get worse before it got better. Twenty-year-old me told herself she was getting back up on her feet, but in fact I was hurtling down to rock bottom.

Just as I finished decorating the ground floor I bumped into an old acquaintance from school. She was my age and had a couple of kids about the same age as mine too.

'Come over to mine on Friday,' she said. 'Bring the kids.'

A couple of glasses of wine seemed harmless enough, and I could really do with some company, but when I arrived I knew pretty quickly it was going to be a different sort of night. There were quite a lot of other people there.

'Shall we pop to the off-licence to get a bottle of vodka?' she said. So, not a glass of wine then. I don't really remember much else about that night and the many nights that followed.

It breaks my heart to say this now but the upstairs of the house never got decorated and it had no carpet, no nice furniture, no photos. The happy memories I had promised myself never made it up the stairs. Meanwhile, downstairs just got darker and darker. There was no window in the room that joined the kitchen with the sitting room and the teal shade I had chosen for the walls soon turned, in my mind, to a dark green sludge. It was a perfect reflection of the state of me. My mind and body were a mess. I thought cheap vodka and cheap whizz would numb the pain. But both just added to the misery and made everything far worse. Within a few short weeks of moving to this estate I knew exactly where to go for a £10 bag of whizz. Nowadays, providers advertise their wares to children on Snapchat using a five-mile radius on Snapmaps. It's all encrypted, of course, because – as I am repeatedly told – it is data that needs protecting.

Years later I told both the kids about this period of our lives. In detail. I was brutally honest about how awful it was, and I must have told Brianna a hundred times that drugs are disgusting, they form a trail of destruction to get to you and a trail of destruction in your wake. It doesn't matter if you are a stunning skinny model in Monte Carlo or, like I was, a lonely single mother on a sink estate – the chemicals you put in your body are the same and, once they get a hold of you, you will steal, lie, cheat, become paranoid and violent, put yourself in danger and degrade yourself.

When social services did finally come knocking on my door to check on the children, it was in fact my mother, out of a desperate act of love, who called them.

She and I had been kept apart for a long time, but now, I was the one putting a barrier between us. The drugs terrified her; after all, she was still picking up the pieces that her foster kids' addict parents had left in their wake. Alisha and Brett were growing into cute, cuddly, funny toddlers but I couldn't see what was in front of me because I was being constantly sucked into a place of self-pity and misery, going over and over the trauma of the past few years. For Mum, imagining my children in respite care must have broken her heart; it would certainly have broken mine. Mum asked everyone she knew what she should do and was amazed at how many people from all backgrounds had members of their families cursed by drugs. She stood by me but refused to 'help'. She wouldn't take the kids to stay with her because she worried that would encourage me to go on yet another bender. She knew the only thing stopping me from throwing my entire life away was that my benefit money ran out every week, so there was no question of her giving me money. I responded by being foul to her, calling her names and refusing to see her. Despite my terrible parenting, I still wanted to be a good mum and the shame was crucifying me from the inside.

My twenty-first birthday was a mess. As a one-off, Mum had taken the kids for a sleepover so I could go out and celebrate. The following morning, she stood on my door-step with two smiling children and a neatly wrapped gift. I had to open the door, even though I had two black eyes and a blinding hangover. She took one look at me and silently handed over the gift.

'Here are your children,' she said, and then left. It was a book on Buddhism, which she had been investigating as a way to get through this difficult time. Like a fool I never read it, but she had planted a seed that there was another way of living. That seed would eventually take root and grow; it helped me not only become the person I am now but protected me when the worst possible thing happened. But it took a while. I went upstairs and stared at myself in the mirror and cried. I hated what I was looking at, I hated what my mum had seen, I hated my life and the shithole we lived in, but even that was not enough to make me stop.

If carrots weren't going to work, then Mum was tough enough to resort to the stick. It was not long after that she made the brave and sickening decision to call social services. They came round to my house. I didn't have carpet, but I had bread and milk in the fridge, some cereal, basic cutlery; there was light, there was heat. I was given a reprieve and told the kids could stay. I remember sitting in that dark green windowless room and realizing I had to get out. I had got lucky. I might not get lucky again. I left the bread and milk, the crappy furniture, I left the drier that had been kicked in, I packed up our few belongings and, once again, went back to Mum's. I knew I could not return to that house, even for a second. A few years ago, I was offered a job, but the room I would have been working in had no windows. I couldn't take the job. I need to be able to see the sky, the light, the way out.

It wasn't quite Mary Poppins time, but I had taken the first step. We were back at Mum's house, where I went cold turkey off the drugs and felt truly terrible for at least two weeks. I am not sure if I would have managed to stick to it if I hadn't been fortunate enough to have somewhere to go and get support with the children. In 2008, we moved into a private rented two-bedroom ground-floor flat, which was also entirely thanks to my mother. The kids had a bunk bed in one room; I was in the other. There was a small garden for the kids to play in and I enrolled them both in the Busy 0–5s nursery. I still wasn't working, but inspired by Mum and encouraged by the council, I enrolled in what was the Warrington Collegiate to study Art and Design. I kept it together during the week, but at the weekends, I found it hard to resist and sometimes I dabbled. It wasn't as bad as before but it was still messy and the comedowns unpleasant. I got furious at myself for not being able to stop, but by Friday I would feel resentful that I had to take care of two children on my own and, stuck at home, started drinking. I vividly remember sitting on the floor of the flat, silently shouting at myself that I had to stop while simultaneously swigging from a vodka bottle, doom drinking.

I know now that the years between sixteen and twenty had left me traumatized. I believed the negative things about myself, and the anxiety created by feeling constantly unsafe, exacerbated by drugs and alcohol, had damaged me more than I realized at the time. I didn't even know there was such a thing as counselling, which could have helped me heal; instead I got drunk and got worse. I lacked the energy or the confidence to be a good enough mother to two fast-growing, exceedingly energetic children, although it was what I wanted more than anything else in the world. I still didn't have the tools to turn my life around. Then a helping hand came my way. Alisha, now aged four and a half, started primary school and Brett ran along after her to the nursery attached.

'*Like literally!*'

Yes, literally. The nursery was a container attached to the main building, but it was a very happy container. Those few minutes in the playground watching all the children run around changed everything. The equipment is pretty impressive now, but even then, it was great. There was space. It felt happy. It sounded happy. I still love the sound of shrieking children running amok at breaktime. This was my old primary school and, in the crowd of parents dropping off their kids, I recognized a face. Nervously, I approached my old friend from Year 4. I didn't need to be frightened; Vicky was – is – lovely and her daughter and mine became firm friends. They are both called Alisha and they are still firm friends. Then I met Keisha, who was training to become a nurse. And then I met Hanifa, who was training to be a personal fitness instructor. Was the universe trying to tell me something? For the first time in a long while I decided it was time to listen.

The hardest part about getting fit is starting, and I'm not sure I could have done it without Vicky's and Hanifa's help.

Especially Hanifa, who I suspect took me on as her personal project. We would meet at school, drop the kids, take the bus and head to a brilliant gym called Total Fitness. It had a running track, a pool and a kids' zone – this was a place where fitness was a family affair. At first, I could barely look up – I was cripplingly insecure in my plus-size leggings and T-shirt – but Hanifa taught me how to use the equipment, how to warm up and make the most of being there. She taught me the difference between cardiovascular fitness and strength and, almost the most transformative, how to lift weights and bench-press. Unimaginable! Me . . . lifting weights! I discovered I was reasonably good at it and, slowly, really slowly, I felt myself begin to change. The weight didn't drop off me overnight, but the tone of my muscles altered. More importantly, I was finding strength in places that were not visible to the human eye. My confidence grew and, without even realizing what was happening, I started feeling emotionally more, I don't know, maybe wholesome is the word.

Hanifa had taught me a fundamental fact. With more respect for my body, I had more respect for myself, which meant in turn I then gained more respect for my body. The routine she had helped me start became the scaffolding of my week as I built my new life, and was the reason why relapses became a thing of the past. I would not jeopardize my workout by feeling terrible, so drinking in the week stopped and I learned to live with my children while they were awake rather than exist in the twilight hours when they slept. Now when I drank it was because I was out, socializing with friends, having a nice but sensible time. I had a ton more energy, but greater even than my new-found friendships, lifestyle and health, was the relationship I was building with my children. We moved into a privately rented ex-council three-bedroom house, and this time I left all traces of my old life behind. Now I would get up with the kids, eat breakfast with the kids, I would walk them to school, get on the bus, work out, come home, clean the house and then go and get the kids, make tea with the kids, watch telly with the kids, go to bed with the kids. That might sound so boring, but for me at the time it was bliss. On one of those blissful mornings, the kids, as usual, had stopped to look at the flowers and insects, and instead of rushing them along we ended up picking daisies. I put them all along Alisha's braid. I wish I'd done that every morning.

In 2011 Brett followed his big sister into primary school and was adored by everyone. He didn't much like sitting down and would rather run rampant with his friend Jack than attempt any reading or writing. Rather than put him on the thinking seat, his teacher suggested I get his eyes tested. It was irrefutable. Brett was staggeringly short-sighted, which meant that for the first five years of his life his world had been out of focus and fuzzy. When we picked up his first pair of glasses they were as thick as the base of a Coke bottle. He slipped them on to his little face.

'Mum!' he exclaimed, excitedly looking into my face. 'You've got freckles!'

How could I not have noticed the slight clumsiness, the falling off things and into things, the lack of interest in books of any kind? I knew exactly how. Once he had his glasses, he adapted brilliantly and started writing me little notes. *To my mummy, thank you for the love and hope.* No, my precious little one, thank *you*.

I applied for a job cleaning at a local car dealership. I needed money always, but more than that, I knew I personally needed a structure. I cycled three miles to work, cleaned the offices and the showroom then cycled back in time to go to the gym and pick up the kids. It was a new privilege to be able to provide for my family. It was a greater privilege to have the confidence to try. I liked having a sense of purpose and I absolutely loved my job. Genuinely, it was the best job in the world, even though I was 'just a cleaner', as I was overheard saying by my wonderful manager, John Whitlow. John pulled me up instantly.

'You are not *just* a cleaner.' At first I thought he was going to pull me up about the time I also spent chatting, which was quite a lot of time, but he surprised me. 'Esther, you are a valuable part of the team. You matter just as much as anyone else who works here.'

Those words made me feel like I had summitted Everest. I had come so far from the dark depths of the estate, step by painful step, so if I went on Facebook and saw people I used to know refer to me as a big fat bike, it did not fell me. In fact, it encouraged me. I was stronger, I was financially independent, I was a good mother. They couldn't hurt me any more. I would pick up my gym bag and head out.

My salary meant I could start taking driving lessons. My clean, decorated house meant I could have friends over with their kids. I took the kids to Total Fitness at the weekends. I could see them on all the mini-gym equipment while I ran around the track. They both fell in love with gymnastics and were soon trying to outdo one another on the mat. Their supple, strong bodies could do the most terrifying things and I would watch in awe as the forward rolls progressed to cartwheels and the cartwheels progressed to flips, then back flips, then all of them were put together in a whirl of red hair and long limbs ending in a pose on a pinpoint. I think that was possibly the only time Brett stood still, that milli-second at the end of a ruthlessly practised gym routine. When I watched the children I would have to clutch my heart because sometimes it felt as if it might burst with love for them. I had finally discovered a sense of pride in myself too. With help from the truly angelic people I have pur-posely named in this chapter, I managed to stop raising hell and instead build a little sliver of heaven for myself and my children, right here in Warrington.

6

University of Hope

Brett and Jack, his best friend from primary school, were in almost constant trouble, thick as thieves, and equally – what shall I say – hard to contain? They weren't mean, but they were mischievous. Perhaps it was inevitable that his mum Donna and I would become friends. We probably met in the naughty corner. Donna was also a fitness trainer, but she used to be a hairdresser, so I would go to hers and she would cut my hair while the kids played. Brett may have been a handful, but he was my handful, and at home he was a loving, boisterous, happy kid. Looking back, those years, 2011 to 2013, were some of the happiest of my life. I was fitter than I had ever been, stronger mentally, and could properly enjoy my children. One evening, Donna somehow managed to convince me that it was time to break my strict routine and go out for a night on the town. In Manchester. She thought it would be good for me to get out. I preferred staying home. Still do, to be honest. But I am very, very glad I went.

On the night, so that I didn't bottle out, Donna came to collect me. Then we went round to pick up her nephew.

'Esther, this is Wes,' she said as he climbed into the back of the car. I couldn't get a very good look at him without turning around, but I know now that he texted his friend saying that he thought I was fit. God knows what Donna had told him. If this was a set-up, I had no idea. Donna knew me well enough not to mention a guy; the kids came first. We then went and collected the friend Wes had texted and the four of us headed back to Donna's for drinks. Wes came round to the front and opened the car door. He held open the front door of the house too. I'd never had anyone do that for me before.

Continuing to surprise me, Wes offered to make the drinks. He was quiet, but the drink he poured me was lethal. Two thirds spirit, one third mixer. He swears he wasn't trying to get me drunk, he just didn't know how to mix a drink. We all got the train into Manchester and headed to a bar in Spinningfields. Donna was happy getting smashed and I went outside to smoke. Wes came too. I couldn't help but keep noticing his manners. He pulled out chairs, he went to the bar to get the drinks. He was utterly charming and not at all what I had been expecting. I offered him a cigarette, which he took, but it was clear from his first puff he didn't smoke. He was just pretending so he could stay in the smoking area with me.

'So, would you come out with me next weekend?' he asked. 'On a date.'

He was lovely, polite, and we were getting on, but

there was one thing he really needed to know. 'Wes, I've got kids.'

He didn't seem remotely put off. 'I don't mind,' he said. 'And I'm older than you.'

Another shrug and a silent smile. So that was it. We were going on a date.

We stayed too long in town and missed the last train home so had to get the coach. Just before the swerving coach and the many doubles got the better of Donna, she kissed Wes's friend, then looked at us.

'You two have got to kiss now,' instructed a slightly slurring Cupid. We duly obliged, but it didn't last long because Cupid then emptied the contents of her stomach all over Wes's mate's trainers. That put an end to any chance of a double date. Frankly, it was possible our date might not have happened. At our wedding speech, on 22 June 2024, Wes reminded our collected friends and family that when we got off that interminable coach to Warrington I was desperate for the toilet. There were none to be found so I had no choice but to speedily locate some industrial bins down an alleyway.

'Classy!' Wes shouted sarcastically from the other side of the bin. 'I can't wait till we're married.' We've been together ever since, but perhaps my unladylike actions were why he *could* wait – for eleven years and two months, as it happened. It was nice to be proposed to while peeing behind a bin.

One weekend later, Wes picked me up from home, opened the car door and drove me to the Trafford Centre to watch a horror film. It was a terrible film, and not even scary, yet somehow I found myself cuddling up to this perfect gentleman. He wouldn't let me pay for anything, he was kind and shy, he smiled with his eyes and seemed genuinely pleased to be out with me. The following weekend we met at the Peacock pub and I brought Vicky and the kids along. Wes was wearing a Superman cap and went over to help Brett win a prize on a grab-a-toy game. On the fourth attempt the toy was finally firmly held in the claw. Wes dropped it into Brett's little hand. He looked up at Wes, smiling broadly.

'You're my hero!'

And just like that, I was in love.

When I fall, I fall hard, and I thought nothing of telling Wes then and there. Perhaps I am a tad impulsive. Sorry, Bree, you might have got that from me. Wes blinked his big eyes back at me and said nothing . . . Just to make sure he had heard me right, I repeated my declaration of love. Did I mention I might be a tad impatient too? All that time, I was so fearful how my son would turn out that I might have missed a few moments where it was clear that my impulsive, impatient, chatty, friendly, stubborn, energetic, extremely loud child was in fact just like me. Wes seemed a bit hesitant and mumbled something about it being a bit soon – a fact I remind him of on a weekly basis – which instigated a minor sulk from me. Lucky Wes. I also frequently remind him that, despite his awkward silence, I was right: we were perfect for one another and it was obvious to any intelligent individual from the start. Lucky, lucky Wes.

Wes didn't move into our house, but he moved pretty effortlessly into our lives. The kids came first, always, so we stuck to our Monday-to-Friday routine – school, gym, work, tea, telly, bed – and Wes would stick to his. He'd had a full-time job since he'd left college at eighteen. On the weekends we had fun. This was the honeymoon period I'd never had before. Me, Wes and the kids hanging from the monkey bars in the playground at the impressive Elizabethan Walton Hall and Gardens. We would spend hours at the children's zoo there, petting the donkeys and feeding the goats, spotting red squirrels and laughing at the pot-bellied pigs. Ice cream was usually involved. Wes was a natural-born nature lover so happily joined us on the trips to the beaches we had grown fond of. It was easy. Almost as if it was meant to be.

Despite his age, Wes didn't seem wary of becoming part of a family. I soon understood why. Wes's stepfather had come into Wes's life when he was six and became his dad almost overnight so, for Wes, being there was more important than biology – and Wes, from day one, has been there. Wes and his dad are very close, so it was natural for Wes to assume he himself would be welcomed into the space in my family where a dad should be. But the kids and I didn't want or need that role to be filled. If anyone was going to discipline my kids, it was going to be me – they were my responsibility. My mum had been parent enough, tough cookie that she is, so it was natural for me to take that independent position too. I didn't need to get tough on Alisha very often, just watch her in the playground, a group of younger children flocking around her; she was a slightly bossy teacher and role model from an early age. Brett, on the other hand, would be rolling in the mud, sliding down a hill, tearing through a field and generally being a bit much. Wes tried to intervene, but the kids were having none of it. After a few rocky moments, Wes adapted to the job of supporting me while I stuck to the job of parenting. That support for me was profound, precious and, if I sometimes take it for granted, let me say it right here – in print – thank you for everything, Wes. You have taken such incredible care of us all. I especially could not have done the last few years without your steadfastness, love and unwavering support. Being there is more important than biology.

It is Wes's quiet encouragement that makes the most difference to my life. Encouragement that perhaps I didn't realize I needed. I loved my cleaning job, but I had a nagging feeling there was more I could do, so when I suggested going back to college he smoothed the way. I might have left it a bit late to be a doctor, but there was an access to healthcare course at Warrington Collegiate which could put me on the path to becoming a nurse. This time I was being smart about it. It was a two-year course. The plan was I would continue working, attend college and during the first year sit my English GCSE and in the second follow up with maths and my beloved biology. But it was very stressful, and I needed support with my mental health, so I looked up how to take care of myself and found the Calm app. I started practising mindfulness with guided meditations and that is what helped me study hard, continue to work and look after the kids. Wes and mindfulness are my two greatest super-powers. I did the research and applied for the grants that would help me achieve my goals. I think the other reason why education was at the forefront of my mind was because Alisha was fast moving towards the end of primary. I began searching for a house that would put us in the catchment area of King's Leadership Academy. I wanted Alisha to go to a school that encouraged pupils to reach their potential. I did not want my children to give up on their education as easily as I had. In fact, I was determined they wouldn't. I wanted them to succeed. As they both progressed through school, I started to feel my own lack of education more keenly. I am sure it was all in my head, but I felt 'less than' everyone else, and I didn't enjoy the feeling. Too many bad memories of being belittled. I believed my boss when he said I wasn't 'just a cleaner', but I needed, for my sense of self-worth, to prove that I was capable of more.

The house we moved to was next to a small station and across the road from a lovely little green with a Scout hut. It wasn't a busy road, but occasionally cars would speed down it and I carried this horrible thought that something bad was going to happen to the kids. I knew I was more nervous than most, and I knew why, but I couldn't rationalize the feeling. It really plagued me. I had nearly lost the kids, and now the thought of how close I came was crippling. I was definitely overprotective as a result. I wouldn't let them play on the green and instead insisted they play in the back garden. I made sure their friends came to ours, and we had lovely, fun summer evenings on the deck at the top of the garden. Mum had given the kids an iPad – another thing to worry about, with Brett's tendency to break things – and among the many family videos there is extremely unattractive morning-after-the-night-before evidence of our nights in the garden with Vicky and the kids.

It was a big garden that rose steeply up a bank edged by huge mature trees at the top, presumably lining the old railway. All the time I was trying to put the brakes on the kids, they were finding the most dangerous ways to play. Brett was constantly climbing those trees. I definitely recall receiving a phone call from Wes telling me I'd better come home, there had been a bit of an accident. Brett was bleeding profusely from the head after falling head-first out of the tree. I took him to hospital, but he didn't seem that bothered. He quite liked the attention, I think.

I don't remember who gave my wildly adventurous children the old four-wheel pram, but they would spend hours pushing it up the hill to the top of the garden then pushing each other back down the hill at breakneck speed. I couldn't watch. It was around this time that my mother's relationship with one of her foster sons got so draining and depressing that she gave up fostering altogether, rented out her house and went off travelling around Mexico. She did it so she could reset her life, knowing that if she stayed she would continually be faced with his increasingly dark and drug-fuelled world. Eventually she got a job in Guatemala where she was able to 'recover' from the broken relationship. We can't do that any more; we can block people and make our social media profiles as private as is possible, but if you have a phone in your pocket, the world goes with you.

I enrolled Alisha and Brett at Bruche Primary. It was quickly clear that Brett was not going to be easily reined in. He could no longer run amok as he had at preschool, and considerably more was being asked of him. Things he found hard to do. To be honest, even basic requests, like sitting down – were proving challenging. It was a teacher who suggested that he got tested for dyslexia. Brett, we discovered, had a quite profound difficulty processing letters and numbers. I thought he had fallen behind because I had missed the fact that he needed glasses. The school tried to reassure me at first. Many kids are dyslexic, they were very used to helping children with dyslexia and I was not to worry or beat myself up. However, it also transpired that on top of poor eyesight and now dyslexia, there was a problem with his ability to track the words on the page.

'Like literally!'

They tested the saccadic movement of his eyes – this is the superfast adjustment our eyes make as we change the fixed points we are looking at. They should be rapid and in sync. Instead, Brett's eyes jumped randomly and in uncoordinated patterns, making reading and writing – already very hard – basically impossible. Suddenly Brett's disinclination to sit at a desk and practise phonics made total sense. I felt terrible. I think I started feeling terrible most of the time when it came to Brett and school. He was given coloured overlays and extra time, and at home he continued to be his energetic, joyful self, but at school something wasn't working and he kept getting into trouble. Vocabulary wasn't a problem – he could talk all four legs off a donkey, usually during class – but if he was asked to put those words to paper, he'd soon give up and cause a distraction. I started to get calls at work. Then one day Alisha came home upset from school. Her form teacher was known to be super strict, so Brett had been brought into Alisha's classroom and told in front of everyone to sit still and not distract Alisha or her classmates.

'Look how embarrassed your sister is!' the teacher said. Brett was gutted. Alisha was furious. Don't get me wrong, she found the non-stop chatter and constant antics deeply annoying, but say a bad word about Brett and you'd see the metal that runs through the core of my elder child. She was his protector and comrade from the start. I went back to school for yet another meeting.

'What do you want me to do?' I asked the teacher before bursting into tears of frustration. I could only manage Brett when I had him; what was I supposed to do from work when he was at school? Was this the time he'd been caught taking things from the classroom? Or the time he'd come in from the playing field covered in mud and grass stains? Or the time he'd answered back? I couldn't tell you. I wish I had tried harder to understand the cause of the disruptive behaviour rather than focus on the behaviour itself. I think I still felt judged as a young single mother, but outside of school Brett and Alisha were both so sweet and such a delight, it was hard to work out what was happening.

'He isn't like this at home,' I repeatedly pleaded. At home, I had the kids under control. Alisha would tell you that she thought I had a superpower for knowing when she and Brett were plotting something foolhardy or dangerous, which, to be fair, was most of the time. It wasn't a super-power, but my spider sense picked up on silence. Silence meant something was on the verge of going horribly wrong. I don't think they believed me.

How many times did I leave a meeting at school, get Brett in the car, and then tear a bloody strip off him? Usually the whole way home. I wanted him to be better, behave better, I wanted him to do as he was told, why couldn't he just sit still and listen? I came down hard on that kid because I was afraid of who he might become, maybe even more afraid of being thought of as a bad mother. Yet here I was, being a bad mother. The feeling of not being good enough made its insidious creep up my spine. I had to be tougher. I had to work harder. I had to do better. Fear and shame. It is a hopeless place to live. The child I was shouting at was the same child that when we went to the doctor to collect his inhaler – yes, he suffered with asthma too – asked the doctor for a hug on the way out. It was as if, in Brett, I had two completely different children.

I thought joining the Scouts would help his confidence, and he was offered the chance to go camping. As usual, he got wildly overexcited when he was there and helped himself to gallons of cordial, which we never drank at home. The sugar made him hyperactive and the following day I got a call. Could I please come and collect him; he was, as ever, a bit too hot to handle. Even for the Scouts. He was miserable when he got home and refused to ever go back. When I unpacked his stuff I found his sleeping bag soaked through. I felt so sorry for him – everything just seemed to go wrong. We tried again when the whole year group went on a residential camping trip. Then the phone call.

'Ms Ghey, could you come and collect Brett? He's . . .'
I can't remember what he'd done this time. Once again I

drove him home, away from the fun and his friends, who he loved so, so very much that he could never contain his excitement. What can a child conclude if wherever he goes and whatever he does he gets into trouble? I watch the videos that the kids made on the family iPad, and all I hear is laughter and glee. I see incredible gymnastics and impressive acrobatics, determination and concentration, and I love them, but it makes me so sad for this happy little kid who could backflip down a hill but always seemed to land himself in big trouble.

One day I came home to find people traipsing around our cottage. Unbeknownst to us, the owners had put the house on the market and I was suddenly in the position of having to find us somewhere new to live – again. And fast. I put our name down for a council house, and waited. It was really stressful not knowing if we had somewhere to go that would keep us in the catchment area for the school I really wanted Alisha to go to. Finally, during the summer of 2015, we were offered a housing association property. It was a total wreck of a place, but by the time I had finished with it, it was perfect. Luckily, my college term had ended so I was able to take two weeks off work to redecorate the entire house. From top to bottom this time. I sanded, I stripped walls, I primed and painted, I wallpapered and washed and, this time, I finished it. Of the many places I have lived in, this housing-association house is the one I loved the most. I worked flat out to make it feel like home. We were finally settled. There are so many heavenly photos of that time. The kids painting (on my clingfilmed dining table), Brett at the keyboard my mum had kindly given to them. He played with two fingers, but he wasn't bad. As ever, his sheer enthusiasm got him quite a long way.

I was so proud of Alisha when she got a place at the highly sought-after King's Leadership Academy and she looked so smart in her blazer and tie as she headed off to her first day of school. I could not have been more proud. Have I said that already? Over the following year we both knuckled down. I completed my access course at Warrington Collegiate and gained good enough grades in maths and biology to fill in a UCAS application. Alisha survived her first year of secondary school, made some nice friends and seemed to be able to cope with the pressure. Like my mum, I had got there a little later than most, but I got there. Alisha was on a more secure educational path and I was proud of her. Can I say it enough?

Our family album is full of moments that are so precious I would like to climb into each of those pictures and stay there a while. I would throw imaginary tomatoes at my children while they locked themselves in the stocks at a National Trust castle. I would ride the merry-go-round with them. I would creep into the hollow of a giant oak in the woods and hide. I would admire them each time they dressed up. I would applaud every gym or dance routine they recorded on the iPad. In one of those videos you can hear me shouting at the kids to be careful . . . not of themselves, but of the iPad. I knew exactly what they were doing on our family iPad. I had every parental control on it and it was password protected. And when they had exhausted themselves and I had finished the washing-up, we would cuddle up on the sofa, Brett in his Pokémon PJs and Angry Birds dressing gown, Alisha in her pink dressing gown and fluffy slippers, and they were the very best of moments.

This is what I notice the most when I scroll through the photos: he is always – *always* – smiling. The kids had a little pink telly and we would often dance around the house to our favourite movie at the time, *Sleeping Beauty* – Alisha with her Disney-princess hair, Brett with tights on his head, me and Wes. We had many such 'Once Upon a Dream' moments. When Wes and I got married, that is the music we walked out of the registry office to. It takes me back immediately to when life was great. My children were happy. We were safe.

My thirtieth birthday was around the corner, and Wes surprised me with a trip to Amsterdam. I could not get over how far I had come since my miserable twenty-first. What next, I wondered to myself. What would the next decade bring? The government had withdrawn grants for nursing, which made nursing financially unreachable for me, so I had to re-evaluate what I wanted to do. After looking at different university courses I decided to go for nutrition, because I figured that instead of giving people medication for illnesses they had developed, I could be part of preventing people getting ill in the first place. I knew from personal experience how much better I felt now that I ate well, exercised and took care of myself. In fact, I had become extremely anti-medication. Nothing like the zeal of a former self-medicator. We didn't even have paracetamol in the house, and I stood by the mantra that there were few things that weren't improved by a glass of water and going outside.

I was excited when I pulled off the M62 and headed into Liverpool. I turned left down Childwall Priory Road and took it as a good omen, as a person prone to anxious think-ing, that it was pronounced 'chilled wall'. The next thing I knew, Hogwarts appeared before my eyes and, just like that, I fell in love again. I could not believe a place of learn-ing could look so lovely. It was incredible – there was a fully equipped sports centre free to use for students, there were cafés and open spaces and, when I took a seat in the lecture hall, it seemed the head of admissions stood on the stage and spoke directly to me.

'Here at Liverpool Hope University we will help you move forward and empower you to build and change your life. Hope is in our name, and hope is what we believe in.'

I burst into tears in that hall because I knew in my heart that this was where I was supposed to be. I also knew it had taken nearly losing my children to start the long journey to bring me to this point. I wanted to be a student of the University of Hope. I wanted to harness the power I had used to change my life and do something positive with it.

7

Detention, Correction, Detention

In September 2018, Brett started secondary school with a fresh blazer, a smart tie, an immaculate precision-cut short back and sides and a brand-new phone. He was a very excitable eleven-year-old following his beloved sister to big school. New friends. New phone. New building. New phone. New drive to school. New phone, new phone, new phone. From the very beginning he would walk around with it in his hand, as if he was the bees' knees, performing and pulling faces, but always with a smile on his face. I thought it was funny. We had 'the chat'. The chat that most parents I know have drummed into them. Talk to your children about what not to do. Have parental controls installed and up to date. I did all that – well, I did what I could. Maybe I did what I thought was all I had to do. I am absolutely certain about one thing: I had no idea about what I was putting into my children's hands. But there had been no issue with Alisha and her phone, and it needed to be fair.

The family iPad my mum had given the kids was a hallowed item, respected, revered and looked after. It was also monitored by me and was always given to me at the end of every day. I was more worried about the iPad being broken while the hundredth backflip video was made and rewatched than what it could bring into our home, and anyway, the parental controls on our Wi-Fi took care of that. So we were safe from potential phishing or grooming or harmful content – or any of the other things I had heard about but did not think applied to me. I admit – before anyone tells me online – that yes, I was extremely naïve about putting such a powerful device in my child's pocket and letting them walk out of the house with it. If I thought about it at all, and I am not sure I did, I was happy to go with the flow, and the flow was that kids went to secondary school with a phone so they could be in contact with their parents about their whereabouts and getting home. I gave the kids phones to help me keep them safe. Oh, the irony. It would almost be funny if it wasn't so tragic. Brett started a new school that had high ideals, many rules and ambitions to hit stellar results, with a new world in his pocket that had low ideals, no rules, but was equally ambitious to hit stellar results. There was a seismic shift in Brett's young life, and looking at photos of him in his new uniform, smiling proudly on his first day of school, well . . . words fail me.

'Year 7, please line up.'

The paint had not long dried on the corridors of this incredible new school, which had clearly been designed and built around pupil achievement. The school was focused on creating good habits in the students and ensuring they adhered to discipline, and that meant sticking to the rules. Blazers had to be worn at all times, even in the summer, except in the classroom, when they could be removed, but only if underneath the student was wearing a long-sleeve shirt. Even the architecture was designed around focus, attention and results. The playground areas for each part of the school were divided by the classroom blocks. And there was absolutely no talking when the kids walked between them. Being respectful to the teachers was of paramount importance because respect for others and their surroundings engendered self-respect, which engendered respect for others, which engendered . . . you get the picture.

'Walk in single file on the left and no talking.' Even Alisha, my 'good' kid, had trouble with that one. I guess I hoped that Brett would follow suit and largely fall in line.

Tablets were handed out to each child so they could complete and hand in homework electronically, and each pupil was expected to reach for their highest possible academic standard. This school was offering its pupils cutting-edge-quality education, and I could not have been happier dropping off my smartly turned-out children before driving to Liverpool to attend uni. My kids weren't going to miss out on an education like I had. There was going to be no backchat, no absences, no opting out, no disrespecting the teachers, no absolving of responsibility and no giving up on themselves before they discovered what they were capable of. What was I thinking? I was thinking that I was doing the right thing, giving them both the best possible start in life. I was thinking of the benefits of aspiration and achievement and self-awareness and professionalism. I wanted the kids to believe in themselves and have integrity and respect for themselves and others, and I was absolutely sure this was the place to make all that happen. On paper it was perfect.

In November, Brett turned twelve, and all seemed to be going well. He was still my happy child who could eat a Dairy Milk as big as him, and although I knew it wasn't plain sailing, nothing appeared out of the ordinary. He shied away from sports, preferring to hang out with girls in the playground. He and Alisha still spent a huge amount of time creating routines. They became shorter and more dance orientated than the intricate gymnastic routines from before, and there was more music involved. I could hear it around the house. I'm sure I'm biased, but the standard was high.

Alisha had a tight-knit group of friends, and soon Brett found his own friends who shared the same interests and would happily create dances together. Soon my avid little YouTuber found new platforms to invest his time in, the iPad became surplus to requirements and in a pretty short period of time the phone became king. What was wrong with making short videos lip-synching to songs while performing a routine? What was wrong with sharing those mini videos with their friends? The kids loved it, and it was only dancing. How bad could dancing be? They were sharing them on a social media app called Musical.ly. I thought it was fun. I wasn't concerned at all.

My rules at home held fast. At the end of every day, before we started getting ready for bed, they would hand me their phones and I would keep them safely on the shelf in my room, switched off, until morning. I wasn't a big social media user myself and would occasionally check in with Facebook and had Instagram but didn't use it religiously. I had no idea that Facebook had bought Instagram and now boasted over a billion users. And I definitely did not know that ByteDance had bought Musical.ly and merged it with another user-generated content platform called TikTok and were racing to catch up. I don't think anyone outside of Meta or ByteDance knew that the number-one objective of those companies was to keep their billions of users online because the more time they spent online, the more data these companies could accrue and the more targeted advertising revenue they could pull in. Billions of users meant billions of dollars, and TikTok caught up and hit that target of one billion users faster than any other company in the short history of the internet.

I thought I knew enough about technology to look over their phones every evening and check nothing bad was happening. I was quite pleased with myself because I could see if the kids had deleted stuff so I would know if they were trying to hide anything from me. I felt pretty sure I had eyes on them, and things were under control. My main concern was that they might speak to a person they didn't know or see something they weren't supposed to, because I knew adults could follow kids and vice versa, and even I knew age verification was laughable. I was not in any way worried about the intense corporate competition that existed inside and between these companies. Because what did that matter to me? I was not afraid about the engagement model they started to chase in order to keep their users 'engaged', because I had no idea that was happening. The tech companies were designing tools to keep users hooked and whoever invented a feature or tool that saw an uptick in user engagement was significantly financially rewarded. Hitting targets meant making money, and there were no defaults set to help teens control their relationship with their phones. In fact, quite the opposite. The whole point was to keep them on their phones for as long as possible. After all, who has the most time to stare at their phones all day? Kids. Current research shows that the age group most abusing screentime are the eleven- to fourteen-year-olds. They spend an average of nine hours a day on a screen but the thing is, I'm not sure they had a chance. The moment the platforms invented a way to personally recommend then automatically start the next clip, it became almost impossible to switch off.

New features on these 'social media' platforms came thick and fast. Musical.ly's hard-won 'Crowns' became ticks. Backgrounds became filters. Both went live. One minute became sixty minutes. You can now 'tip' your favourite content creator, you can split your screen, you can film something alongside another video, and all of it can be uploaded and downloaded, shared and sent and re-sent and tweeted and retweeted, and all the time you are watching, watching, watching, they are selling, selling, selling, the views are building, building, building and suddenly every kid could become that lucky Instagrammer or TikToker with a million views and a million likes and a million pounds in their back pocket. It's genius, really – every child became a content provider and consumer simultaneously. Now, Brett, would you please sit down and do your physics homework?

We hit our first road bump, like many others do, with a case of peer-on-peer bullying. Brett was friends with a group of girls who were constantly having fights and falling out. So far, nothing new. In this instance, the bitchiness continued long after the kids had gone home. I can't remember why this poor girl was being picked on that week, but everyone was putting their oar in and it was getting seriously mean. Then someone added her to the group chat so she found out exactly what was being said about her. I don't know if it was to help this child discover her friends were not her friends or to humiliate her at an extra-grotesque level; either way, she was devastated. The parents must have seen the comments, or the girl showed them, I can't remember, but they quite rightly went straight to the school. I was called in. This was my first experience of a WhatsApp pile-on.

There were 'games' to be worried about too. A letter from school arrived, and this time it went to everyone. There was a challenge circulating on WhatsApp that hit the media and soon went viral, or went viral then hit the media. We were told there had been extreme examples of this challenge resulting in self-harm and, in extreme cases, accidental suicide. I know now it wasn't the first horrible challenge that kids were encouraged to follow online, and it wouldn't be the last. I am part of the Bereaved Families for Online Safety group, and three people on that group lost their sons to a completely out-of-the-blue suicide. The shock those deaths detonated in each family was beyond comprehension.

Without looking into the details too much, I did speak to the kids. I warned them the challenge was potentially dangerous and not to engage with it. I could see Brett's ears prick up as I was saying it. Something I shouldn't do? That sounds interesting. And I knew if he hadn't already seen this stupid, horrible, insidious challenge, he soon would. Be careful, I warned, though I wasn't sure of what. Talk about being caught between the devil and the deep, dark, drowning sea.

*

The school day at King's was long, so when I pulled up out-side the school, Alisha often appeared exhausted, climbed into the car, desperate to get home, eat tea and collapse on the sofa. On this day we were catching up in the car so I didn't notice that five minutes had become ten, ten became fifteen. I rang Brett's phone. No reply. After half an hour Brett appeared. He had been given a correction, which was basically a detention, for talking. I think we all scoffed a little at the ridiculous rule of no talking in the corridor as we drove home and scoffed again that during his correction he had to write out the aspirations of the school. It was not a red flag. It was just an irritant. Until it happened again.

Support for Brett came from his science teacher. I think he recognized in Brett something of himself and took him under his wing. He made an extra effort to connect with Brett, and his belief in positive affirmation seemed to be working.

It goes without saying that I was absolutely delighted Brett had a genuine supporter inside school. It appeared the course correction had worked, because by April the next year he seemed to be making better choices for him-self. In an email, Brett was congratulated for concentrating, participating and not allowing himself to be distracted. Emails like that were gold dust, and I valued them accord-ingly. It meant that, under the right conditions, Brett could succeed at school. His science teacher asked me to reaffirm to Brett how pleased everyone was with him.

I did try, but by the summer term things had started to deteriorate. I must have not tried hard enough, I must have let my frustration that we were going backwards show. That's what I've beaten myself up about since Brianna's death, but now I think that an alternative lifestyle was dangled in front of Brett, then recommended and pushed by a network of digital algorithms that meant if you like this, Brett, then you'll love this; and if you love this, then you'll be obsessed by that; and if you're obsessed by that, then it would appear that a life was on offer that did not include homework or school or rules, for that matter, and people would just pay you to unbox free gifts and try them on, or worse. But I didn't know any of that at the time. All I knew was that Brett was in trouble again.

One day, Alisha's favourite teacher scooped her dejected brother up and sat him down in the art room. Brett did a painting that the art teacher was so impressed with that she deliberately went to find Alisha to let her know. It wasn't easy being the sibling of the kid who was always in trouble and, since he confided in her, and only her, she carried a heavy burden of worry and love for her brother. That painting hangs on our kitchen wall and is one of my most treasured possessions. It is a homage to Mr Kipling's exceedingly good cakes, a stunning watercolour of pinks and purples. Brett turned thirteen in November and his cake was pink, decorated with the pink French Fancies that he loved, with extras on the side. One thing the Ghey family can agree on: you can never have enough exceedingly good cakes and, if they are pink, the more the better. Brett is smiling in the photo. It was a happy, sweet moment. He was still my Brett, my baby. Maybe the teenage years had started a bit early, but we would be okay. Cake helped.

Finally, though, I had to admit to myself that this prestigious school was not the place for my effervescent child. Birchwood High School, the secondary school I had had to leave because of my own poor behaviour, loomed back into sight. At the very least he could get himself home after detention, because it was only a fifteen-minute walk from where we lived. It started me thinking, and by 20 December my decision was made. I sent King's an email letting them know that I would be applying to transfer Brett to Birchwood High. My old school would, with luck, be our saving grace.

8

Please God, Not Britney

A new uniform, a new pair of glasses, a new haircut, a new attitude? Well, we would see. Arriving at Birchwood High, Brett looked relaxed, not quite as buttoned up as before, perhaps a bit more everyday, just a kid going off to school in his new uniform. Nothing to see here. I hoped and prayed he would fit in. I knew Birchwood looked after more children with special educational needs than King's did. I hoped Brett would get the help he needed with the challenges he faced every day with the eye-tracking, the dyslexia, his poor vision and his asthma. What I'm saying is there was hope – we were hopeful. Looking back now, I realize he had lasted one and a half terms longer than I had before I moved school. But then the pandemic hit. If I had managed to get him to stay at King's, then maybe it would have all worked out differently. If I had managed to stay at Birchwood then maybe it would have all worked out differently. The *if only*s would poison and corrode my mind if I didn't know how to use mindfulness to help.

Stop, Mum. Don't look back. Look up. If you hadn't moved schools, your life would have gone in a different direction and there would never have been Brianna and you wouldn't have Alisha, and that would have been far, far worse.

I imagine her saying this to me and she's right, of course, so I plant my feet and look up, searching the sky for flecks of pink because since she left us, that is where I find her.

Soon we were all glued to screens as we watched the death toll go up and listened to Boris Johnson telling us that things were more serious than having to wash our hands while we sang 'Happy Birthday'. We would all have to go home and stay home for the foreseeable future. I'd been studying for a long time by then, so when my course went online and my graduation was all but in the bag, I decided to apply for jobs as a new product developer in the food industry. I am not sure if I wanted a job in that industry because it meant I would qualify as a key worker, but I suspect I did.

In April, I started my new job as a product development technologist. So much for preventing illness – I was now designing pie fillings, but I loved it from the start. This is what I had been working towards for a long time, and I felt good about it. My fellow employees were lovely, we all had Covid stories and it was undeniable that the support we offered one another was real and heartfelt. Elderly parents and kids doing home learning were constant subjects of concern. Alisha took her school tablet home and knuckled down. Her GCSEs were that summer. No one knew what was going to happen, but mocks were suddenly even more important. Brett, on the other hand . . . oh my God, talk about pulling a horse to water. He bucked and bolted. There was no way I could get him to drink. There were more interesting things to find online than fractions. Such as *Minecraft*. YouTube. Snapchat. House Party – on which you could talk to all your friends. The emails from school started almost as soon as lockdown did. But it was okay, it was only going to be a couple of weeks; after the Easter holidays we could restart, back at school. Surely after this small false start my child would settle down and get to work.

The Easter holidays ended, and no one went back to school. Now what the hell was I going to do? GCSEs were cancelled and the sun came out, so Alisha went for long walks with her friends and had a reasonably nice time, all things considered. Brett barely left his room, and the phone never left his hand. Emails from school were landing in my inbox with alarming regularity. Brett had not turned up to online lessons. He had not even pretended to be online, like many others. He simply could not be bothered and couldn't understand what the fuss was all about. When I tried to confiscate his phone, all hell broke loose. I can't remember the first hole that was punched in the wall, and I don't remember the last. We were entering into a new phase where holes in walls became our normal. If I managed to get his phone off him, he simply took it back. If I hid it, he broke things. If I went into my room to let him calm down, he followed me in digitally, *ping, ping, ping*. It was relentless and wearing. Work was a nail-biting thirty miles away, so if he messed about at home, I was too far away to intervene and, frankly, it wasn't Alisha's job or her responsibility. Brett missed his friends from King's, and he hadn't had time at Birchwood to make new ones. The sole draw of school was friends, and now there wasn't even that on offer. He retreated further online. He wasn't miserable to start with because, although he was up in his bedroom on his own, he wasn't alone. In fact, he was very busy with his new obsession: hair and make-up. I began to notice that the only joy coming back to his face was when he discussed a new make-up trend or the beauty influencers and tutorials he loved to watch on YouTube. As we moved glacially through summer, Brett started actively growing his hair. His sister had hair that would make the Little Mermaid envious and since he had always idolized her, it didn't feel anything out of the ordinary. In fact I was happy for him to try, and it suited him.

The continued refusal to join any online lessons seemed to bleed into the rest of our lives. Brett seemed reluctant to come out of his room and join us, too, after a while. It really bothered me, and after another foul argument about screentime I took his phone off him and told him he wasn't getting it back for two weeks. For the first few days it was like watching an addict go through cold turkey. He was awful, agitated, pestering, needling and grumpy. But after a couple of days there was a change in him. It felt like the dark clouds that had hovered over him started to lift, he left his room, he joined us at the kitchen table, his cheeky-chappy chat came back. I didn't see it as a punishment, I saw it as a gift. When we went on holiday he happily spent time with us, joining us on daytrips and splashing about in the hot tub in the forest lodge we rented. We had a laugh swanning about in our matching towelling robes. I was so happy – it felt like I had my kid back – but then the holiday came to an end, we headed home and the pestering started again. In three days I'm getting my phone back . . . in two days . . . today! As soon as he had that damned thing back in his hand, he was up to his room.

'Mum,' said Alisha, 'a heads up. Brett thinks he might be trans.' It was like when she told me he was gay: it seemed obvious the second she'd said it, but a second before I hadn't noticed. Your children are just your children and you love them as they are, even when you're yelling at them.

'Don't worry,' Alisha said. 'Brett has done a lot of research.'

Of course he had. When he found a subject he was interested in, he went all out. That's how he got so good at backflips. That was how he'd perfected a pencilled eyebrow arch. Brett came downstairs and told me, 'I want to live as a girl.'

'Okay.'

'I'd like my pronouns to be she and her.'

'Okay.'

'Okay.'

I wasn't shocked; in fact, it felt easy, like things were beginning to fall into place. My only concern was when Brett started listing the medications that were needed.

'Hang on, medication?'

The list was long and well researched, but it was medication. I had spent three years learning about the healing power of foods; I was and still am anti-medication. So I pushed back. A bit. 'Why don't we change your wardrobe first and see how you feel?'

I was rewarded with a smile. I watched all that nervous energy take on a new shape. Agitation became excitement, and honestly, just like that, she seemed transformed. In that moment it felt like, together, we could take our first baby steps into this new world which might be able to give my child some peace and joy. She really did look happy as she bounded back up to her room. Of course I was also worried for her, concerned about how this would happen, perplexed about how she would be received outside our safe haven, but I was fully prepared to go on that journey with her, and from the beginning, following in Alisha's footsteps, I completely supported her decision.

With Brett's renewed vigour and purpose, her phone became a portal to a new, exciting world. She was going to become like the people she followed. She was going to become TikTok famous and it was going to solve all her problems. No wonder she bounded gleefully upstairs. All those feelings of not being good enough were going to vanish in a puff of pink powder and all would be well. She was still only thirteen, she was young at heart and in mind, and perhaps she thought we could wave a magic wand and make a princess appear. She *would* go to the ball. She still spent a lot of time in her room, telling us she was talking to her friends, though I had no idea who they were and I never met them.

Part of me had thought it was normal for a kid to be on their phone that much – well, normal-ish for a kid during an abnormal pandemic – but I had to admit to myself that with Brett there was something worrying going on. Alisha could put her phone down, I could put my phone down. Brett could not. People say the internet is helpful for vulnerable people, and yes, I think Brett *was* vulnerable at this point, perhaps had always been, because she had lived a long time on the peripheries, not quite fitting in, but now the online world offered her a place where she could belong. I realized that she was searching for something that would make her feel better about herself and was happy she had found it, but she still needed boundaries, she still needed protecting and she still needed to put her phone down sometimes and be a part of our family. I felt like I was the annoying nag who was getting in her way.

*

Brett spent hours locked away with her phone and I had noticed that the agitation had returned. Sometimes she was hyper, sometimes she was miserable; in either state we were in conflict. At first it was only ever around the phone and her attitude to it, but soon it wasn't just the phone. It was the games console too. We did not have the latest interactive kit which Brett really wanted. And unlike her phone, I could dismantle the console and remove it if she stepped out of line. Like parents all over the world, behaviour chips for access to the internet, games, friends and social media became an incessant bargain and constant haggle. If you do a, b, c, you can have 30 minutes, 1 hour, 90 minutes. I would stand firm but Brett was relentless when she wanted something. Relentless. If only she could have a console of her own . . .

Then she was offered one from someone we used to know and she jumped at the chance, against my wishes. But after meeting up with this person, it became clear the offer of the new PS4 was too good to be true. I am proud to say that when Brett was told *I* should have got her that expensive games console, she defended me, saying it was her behaviour that resulted in the one we had being confiscated, and that was on her and not on me. Brett had fought me tooth and nail for access to the internet so it was music to my ears when she told me what she'd said – because it meant one important thing: deep down she knew, had always known, that I had her best interests at heart.

I know things continued in a downward spiral from this

point but, still, I hold this knowledge close to my heart. We would have got there in the end. I just had to stand firm. The boundaries I insisted on became battle lines and the skirmishes were hardcore, but I believe she knew that whatever side of the line she was on, she was loved by me.

The next day nasty voice notes from this person began to arrive – which I thought were pretty hard for a child to hear, so she blocked contact – but not before I had recorded and kept every single one.

The thing is, the promise of a PS4 was taken at face value. It was simple. Go to a shop and buy one. If you don't, then you're full of shit. It was always black and white with Brett; there was little nuance or social finessing. I had seen it all her life. Thoughts that most people held back, she did not. She had no filter. I used to think it was because she liked to create havoc; now I wonder if she simply didn't recognize the havoc she caused. Either way, it had got her into trouble her whole life and, if you knew Brett at all, you knew that. I used to put it down to enthusiasm, excitement, exuberance, but lately I had been wondering if something else wasn't going on.

For a while Brett did seem more grateful and less hostile towards me, but I think it all must have cut quite deep. This was one of the first people Brett had met, in person, since identifying as she/her, and the blowback was vicious. I think she masked rejection with humour. She laughed it off.

She would do a lot of laughing from this point on. It was not always a happy sound. She retreated to her room and to the ever-present comfort of her phone, which I thought was proving to be less and less of a comfort.

In August we had a meeting in the school library, socially distanced, to discuss uniform for when school returned in person. Brett was adamant that she would only wear the girls' uniform. She looked amazing though, and I rather loved the blonde wig we had bought her while her hair grew. She was also getting very good at doing her make-up. One day she was recognized in the shopping centre by someone who had seen her online, and she looked fit to burst. However, and this is why it was so complex, she was shy too. Shy about being looked at too closely, shy about being seen, and like every unlucky teenager I know, she hated her spots.

The uniform meeting went well and the school agreed that she could wear the girls' uniform. Brett was nervous about going to school in person, but I think she was excited too. She was getting more and more followers, and although it was a little pond, she was getting to be a medium-sized fish. Birchwood Community High School welcomed her with open arms and I was so pleased that I emailed the school to let them know that no one had been mean, that her fears had been unwarranted and that she was actually happy to go in each day. I was so relieved. Our transitions from one school to another, from lockdown to release, from him to her, had all been a success. I thought we'd done it.

Then the emails started. The problem at Birchwood wasn't the school or her peers, the problem was Brett's behaviour. By October I had a printout of all the lessons she had disrupted, all the uniform infringements she'd been pulled up on, and the number of times she'd been caught with her phone in class.

'I don't want to go to school at all,' she announced.

'I'm going to be TikTok famous,' she said.

'School is pointless,' she declared. 'I didn't go before, so why do I have to go now?' There was no getting through to her, and by now she was slipping so far behind academically that I didn't think she would ever catch up.

'Honestly, Brett, what do you want?'

'I don't want to be Brett any more.'

Okay.

'I want to be called Blossom.'

Was she goading me or being serious? Thankfully, Alisha was there to break the tension.

'That sounds like a stripper's name.'

That was a cue for Brett to strike a pose, but she readily agreed. Not Blossom.

'What about Britney?'

'Please God, not Britney,' I said, daring to smile.

'Agreed. There is no way I am calling you Britney,' piped up Alisha.

'I want to keep the B though.'

Okay. We sat down to draw up a list. It was like choosing names for a baby, and I suppose in a way, though I didn't know or fully understand it at the time, I was giving birth to a new child and losing my old one. Bridget. Briony. Bella. Bree.

'Brianna?'

Brett looked at me and smiled.

'Brianna,' she said. 'I like that.'

Honestly, I think that was the only time in our entire lives that she willingly compromised on anything. Ever.

Like literally!

9

Stop Saying That

Brianna was beautiful. That's not just a proud mother talking, she really was amazing-looking. Brianna took a lot of work to perfect and polish. One morning I could hear her talking loudly in her room. She hadn't made it down for breakfast so I walked into her room.

'You're going to be late.'

'Get out! You're messing up my live.'

Your what? 'Who are you talking to?'

'Go away!'

She was really cross and embarrassed. I was cross and alarmed. After that, her 'get ready with me' would become a daily ritual. The foundation, the sculpting, the shading, the bronzing, the I don't know what, and nor did I know who was watching this fourteen-year-old schoolgirl getting ready in her bedroom every morning. I worried that it wasn't other fourteen-year-old schoolgirls. When I tried to ask her, it did not end well. The numbers of people following her were increasing. Whatever she was doing, it was working, and she liked it. Brianna was coming into her own: she was getting more and more followers and she was getting really good at her 'transition' vlogs.

I was happy for her, of course, but I wasn't quite as enthusiastic about the online stuff. When she got shitty comments (*'Call that a natural look, Brian?'*), she would tell me and Alisha, laughing it off. She claimed she didn't care as long as her numbers kept building. Her goal remained steadfast: she would become TikTok famous and no amount of mean comments was going to stop her. She didn't hold back either. Brianna was more than capable of replying with cutting comments of her own, calling people out for being ignorant or – the worst – old! But for all Brianna's sass, and there was plenty, I started to feel a nagging concern. On the one hand, Brianna's 'look' was getting more childlike and cutesy, with pigtails and pink heart emojis; on the other, it was getting more adult. Any steer from me and we would clash. I didn't know what I was talking about. I knew nothing. At the same time, her room was getting really untidy, she started skipping showers and sometimes she forgot to brush her teeth. It was almost as if the more time she spent preening herself, the less she noticed the mess she was creating. The more self-care videos she was making, the less care of herself she was taking. Something was going on, but I couldn't put my finger on it. I ran my concerns past Wes. It was true, she'd been a messy kid, her belongings scattered around the house, constantly losing a sock or a shoe. But when she was little I would tidy up after her. Now when I asked her to tidy her room, she closed the door in my face. Then I'd hear the unmistakeable sound of her phone playing a video. I was just as worried about what she was watching as I was about who was watching her. When she emerged, it was TikTok Brianna, wearing her school skirt provocatively short, lots of make-up and a persona that was being built on social media but with which she strutted into school.

'You're only fourteen.'

'Nearly fifteen!'

'You're going to get into trouble wearing that skirt so short!'

'You're just jealous you haven't got a bum like mine,' she said, and slammed the door behind her. The war of attrition had begun.

'Brianna Ghey.' A teacher pulled her over in the corridor. 'Please roll down that skirt. It is not a belt.'

'You shouldn't be looking, miss.'

'It is school rules, Brianna.'

'You're sexualizing a child. I could report you.'

Brianna was developing a staggering lack of respect for any kind of authority, mine included. I was horrified about the way she spoke to the teachers, especially the ones who from day one had been put in place to support her. If it wasn't the uniform, it was the phone; if it wasn't the phone, it was the nails. When I was called in, which I eventually was, I had to leave work early to drive the thirty miles to school. Brianna would saunter in as if she did not have a care in the world, toss her latest wig, raise her perfectly arched eyebrows and stare into her phone as if none of us were in the room. The teacher seemed a little wary so I spoke up.

'Please, Brianna, put the phone away.'

She didn't even bother looking up. 'No,' she said, and continued scrolling. Since we were there because of the phone, it was pretty provocative. Too provocative. I wondered what she was up to. The teacher tried to come to my rescue, told her not to speak to me in that manner and asked her to put the phone down, but they got the same response. The teacher and I looked at each other silently. I wondered if we were thinking the same thing. When did we become so powerless? She told me afterwards that most of their time was taken up fire-fighting behaviour around phone use.

Is it bad that there was a part of me that welcomed other people being on the receiving end of what I had been dealing with for several months? It is so easy to blame a child's behaviour on poor parenting, it is a natural go-to, but I didn't know how to deal with this situation. I was offered a place on the Teams Around Family (TAF) programme. I grabbed it with both hands. For the first time in a very long while I felt like I would be treated as part of the solution rather than part of the problem. It was a relief to have someone else to tell my worries to other than Wes, my constant support;

Vicky, my dearest and oldest friend; and Flo, my brilliant, long-suffering manager at work. A team who was qualified and who could identify and access help. Pretty quickly we started discussing options. But it wasn't going to be easy because as soon as the school started putting a structure into place that Brianna would have to sign up to and adhere to, she told the teacher overseeing her pastoral care that she was feeling increasingly anxious about even coming into school.

Brianna did not shy away from announcing to anyone who would listen that school was pointless, so wasn't it a little convenient that anxiety would get her what she wanted? To be back at home, on her phone, with no one telling her what to do or, more importantly, what not to do. But the school was more forgiving than me and the reduced timetable Brianna had at first been offered after lockdown, and which she had declined, was offered again. Brianna would be able to pick the lessons she felt able to come in for. Hadn't I pulled that very same trick myself? I was pretty suspicious and adamant that Brianna being at home alone, while I was at work, felt very like lockdown and I mapped the beginning of Brianna's slide into a tech black hole back to lockdown. Surely the best thing for her was to get her back into full-time education and benefit from the much-needed change of spending time with real friends.

I did admit to the school that though making friends had not been an issue for Brianna, keeping them was. I think I was right to push back, although it caused havoc between us, but I was also wrong. I knew it took a lot of physical effort to become Brianna; I don't think I realized how much mental effort it took to be her too. I think she genuinely was overwhelmed by the long days at school performing as proud TikTok Brianna, being the eye-catching girl who could turn heads. People did look up to her and at her, she'd worked hard to make them, but she was never sure why they were looking at her. Was it because they 'liked' her look, or was a comment coming her way that was harder to laugh off in the real world? If a post didn't get many likes, she could delete it. But she couldn't delete herself. Or could she?

Her friends, she said, were being mean online, and I began to notice she would get nervous walking down the street, especially if there was a group of boys hanging around. She would make us detour whereas before she would have stood up for herself. In fact the only time she'd had any sort of verbal abuse at school was from a group of boys. She went straight to the head and reported them, so it was hard to get a handle on this version of Brianna, who seemed as if she wanted to side-step the real world. Alisha told her she was being ridiculous, but maybe even she didn't know everything.

The school accepted that Brianna was struggling and allowed her to start the reduced timetable. They were worried, and supported me getting an appointment with the GP for a referral to CAMHS (Child and Adolescent Mental

Health Services). At this point she'd refused to speak to anyone at TAGS, the trans and gay support group.

I will never know if this growing insecurity about her looks created the anxiety that would cause her to retreat to her room, or if the isolated way she lived online made her so anxious about her looks she found it increasingly hard to leave her room, but from this time on, it felt to me like the two were feeding off each other, and off her. It was as confusing as it was frustrating. Somehow she could filter out her freckles, she could mime to a voice that was not hers, she could sashay, pose and pout, all without revealing the grimy mess in her room or the fear that was building in my fearless child.

If Brianna thought the school was just going to let her do whatever she wanted, she was wrong. She could not wear her uniform however she liked. Or bring out her phone in lessons. Or spend more time making TikTok videos in the toilets than in those lessons. She spent her goodwill tokens rapidly and, before Year 9 was out, Brianna was on a pastoral support plan which meant she had to report daily to the head of school. Over the coming months this was supplemented by a behaviour contract that she had to agree to commit to and, after exhausting the teachers who were assigned to help her with accusations, a risk assessment. The school had to protect their staff as well as their pupils. They tried to do both, and signposted us to all the professional help she could access, but every Teams Around

Family meeting we went to felt further away from that nervous but exciting first meeting in the library. With a waitlist of 300,000 children, any appointment at CAMHS is gold dust and not to be wasted. You don't pick and choose these times, you take them and then make them work. I would race back down the M6, grab Brianna and go in. It takes a lot of effort from a lot of people to get these appointments, and I was relying on them for help, but Brianna had other ideas. She put on her make-up and seemingly without a care in the world told the CAMHS practitioner that she was absolutely fine. Totally fine.

'To be honest, I don't know why I'm here,' she declared. If she said she was fine, what did it matter that I, her mother, said anything different? Brianna told them I was overreacting.

Then she'd flip back. At home, vegging out in her pink fluffy pyjamas, curled up with the dogs, Brianna could suddenly, sometimes, seem more than fine, and I would berate myself again, for worrying *too* much. Maybe the pit in her room didn't matter. It was her room, after all.

'Don't be such a stress-head, Mum.'

All the kids were online; perhaps I *was* overreacting. Brianna could be funny and have us all in hysterics, and as long as I didn't ask her to do anything she didn't want to do – and gave in to most of her demands – she was great. Very occasionally her lovely friend Keira would come over for a sleepover – she was the only friend who Brianna would see in person without full make-up on. With her friend who lived in Scotland, she would spend hours playing *Minecraft*, building little cottages and huge, detailed, pink castles. Every so often there would be a falling-out with both of her friends, as Brianna could say things that weren't particularly tactful, but Keira would always come back and the attempts to put on ridiculously long fake eyelashes would continue, and Brianna would settle her differences with her online friend and they would go back to chatting on Face-Time for hours. I wonder if they realized that Brianna didn't mean to be hurtful, she just missed social cues that others read easily. They were loyal friends but Brianna's truest and most faithful comrade was her sister. I don't think parents ever tire of seeing their children wrapped up in pyjamas, curled up, chatting, and Alisha and Brianna could do that for hours. They would talk about boys, they would talk about make-up – of course – they talked about being uncomfortable in their skin. Even Alisha, who after using filters on her phone was getting a creeping feeling that she didn't like what she looked like without them. The filters could narrow the nose, alter the shape of her face, enlarge the eyes, fill out the lips and airbrush the lot. Even I felt the sharp sting when seeing myself without the softening smoothing effect of a filter. But once the online image had been perfected, the ring light switched off, we all got a nasty shock at the sight of a true reflection staring back at us in the mirror. It is now recognized through research how damaging this is and in December 2024, TikTok admitted as much by placing 'age restrictions' for under-eighteens on some of their beauty filters. I think this just goes to show that they can respond to the needs of certain age and vulnerability groups.

Brianna started looking at herself in the mirror all the time, obsessively, unhealthily. At first I assumed it was because she loved how she looked, but in fact the reverse was true. Brianna started to find faults in her appearance which she got increasingly self-conscious about. There was always something she was unhappy about, that could be fixed for her viewers but not for herself. If I mentioned the link between her feelings and her phone I was called unprintable names. I knew we needed real and effective help before things got really out of hand. Who was I kidding? They were already out of hand.

Brianna was childlike; she was also naïve and would believe whatever she read on TikTok. It led to more fights at home and fallings-out at school in the few hours she was there. I realize now that it made her extremely vulnerable in the online world. The TikTok version of Brianna – who gave as good as she got, could sideswipe you with a look and had not one iota of victimhood about her – was vulnerable too. Amassing viewers was her *raison d'être* (and her reason for 'not needing' an education) and she would do anything to get more of them. She would morph into whoever she was obsessed with at the time, so when she started avidly following an influencer who seemed to promote sex work as an empowering way to make money, my anxiety spiked.

I know now that in 2022 a previously niche fitness and lifestyle vlogger, Andrew Tate, went from berating boys for being loser gamers to creating a terrifying hustle culture that went viral on TikTok after he claimed women should take some responsibility for being raped. Boys loved him. He had 10 million followers and his videos were viewed 13 billion times. His derogatory content couldn't be shut down because he achieved all this without having a TikTok account of his own. What he did was build an army of teenage affiliate marketers by offering them a financial incentive to re-post clips of his videos. Millions of boys started to emulate his attitude and his abs.

According to Jamie Tahsin's documentary *The Man Who Groomed the World*, what came next were courses on how to set up live webcam businesses by first grooming women using his 'loverboy' approach. It follows a pattern I am all too aware of. First the 'love bombing', the compliments and gifts; then the switch, the aggression and isolation. Some women noticed the red flags and got out, but many more do not. The statistics are well known but I would like to repeat them here, for all the women suffering today. Every week in the UK, two to three women are killed by their partners and three more a week take their own lives as they see no other way out. Tech is used to monitor and control; some abusive partners turn down the heating and light remotely just because they can. Whatever the motive behind this behaviour, the outcome is the same. Women are being put in serious danger. The participators of these courses were awarded an Andrew Tate PhD. It stands for Pimping Hoes Degree and consists of basically the same tactics that street pimps use. Just as Instagram has damaged young teenage girls by cultivating insecurity while simultaneously creating an economy of envy, Andrew Tate has singlehandedly skewed the male perspective, legitimized misogyny and normalized the sexualization of women purely for men's gratification and financial gain. Neither are empowering. I think Brianna was being attacked from both sides. She needed time to figure out who she was, away from the garbage playing havoc with her mind. Time she was robbed of. I knew the insecurity she felt was real; what I didn't know then was how vulnerable that made her to be digitally pimped.

Driving to and from work, I used to pass a company where I had applied for a graduate training scheme. I hadn't got the job, but it was a gold-standard workplace and I couldn't help thinking how much easier my life would be if I worked that close to home. I could help Brianna get to and stay in school, I could make sure she never missed an appointment and more importantly it was the only chance I had of monitoring her screentime and use. I loved my job and the people I worked for, but I was stretched beyond breaking point. My prayers were answered and I got a call from them telling me about a New Product Development job opening. I applied, and in August I started my new job, delighted that I would be nearer home to keep an eye on Brianna.

The new job was tougher than I expected it to be. Leaving the close team I had worked with, who knew what I was dealing with at home, made me realize what it is to be supported at work. I worked hard and I always got it done, but when I had to vanish because something had happened at school, my boss at my old job understood and let me go. This new company was different. It worked hard for its reputation as a leader in its field, and I was completely unprepared for the corporate environment. The hours were long and the days were intense, and I missed escaping into the kitchen and working on new flavours and fillings. Now I was stressed at home and stressed at work, and I had lost my support network. For employees with small children, there was some leeway. Everyone understood that, even with the best planning, kids sometimes needed picking up, or were sick, and nativity plays should not be missed. But I had a teenager. My ever-growing fear was that unless Brianna engaged with the support, we wouldn't get any help at all.

So at the CAMHS assessment, I tried to explain, as gently as possible, that she was *not* fine, but every time I spoke Brianna pulled a face. I didn't want to list the filthy room, the lack of hygiene, the holes in our walls, but I had to. Even though it was awful saying it all in front of her. We already had a family support worker who Brianna wouldn't engage with and unless things changed, we wouldn't get any help at all. Those warnings led to a horrible row.

'What's wrong with you! They are trying to help you!'

'No one is trying to help me.'

'All I do is try and help you.'

'I don't need any help! Why can't you just love me the way I am!'

'I do love you. I love you more than life.'

'No you don't, you don't love me.'

'Oh my God, I love you so much. I would die if anything happened to you.'

'I hate you. You don't do anything for me.'

It was maddening. How could she not see how much was being done for her? I felt that we were doing everything and all I was getting was shit. Unfortunately, the CAMHS assessment concluded that Brianna did not need their services and she was discharged. I was on my own again.

We reached a new low in August of that year. Maybe it was because I was putting myself under such pressure to excel at my new job or because, now that I was working closer to home, Brianna felt I should be available to her 24/7. But I wasn't, I couldn't be. I am a hard worker, and my old company had given me a glowing reference. I did not want to let anyone down. I would pull up outside my house at the end of a long day and sit quietly, my hands gripping the wheel, wondering what lay in store for me. It was the holidays and, having refused to engage in any of the services she'd been offered, all she did, every waking hour, day in day out, was be online. She refused to leave the house. I didn't know why the phone was having such a negative impact on her, but I knew it was. Our house is not large; I could hear through the walls the crap she was listening to. It made my blood run cold. Her posts were so obviously suggestive. On one of the few evenings she came downstairs, I tried to address the situation. It escalated rapidly, and she gave me a barrage of verbal abuse. Then she slapped me. Wes was in the next room and rushed in to help, taking Brianna's phone off her. I was so stunned I couldn't move. Brianna ran upstairs and started smashing things up. Wes looked at me. This could not be our new normal.

By this point CAMHS had discharged Brianna. The school appealed their decision on our behalf, telling them that Brianna had not been honest in the meetings, and both the school and I needed that decision overturned. It was investigated, but the decision was upheld, so before term ended, with no official support in place, our TAF contact told us to call the police if things deteriorated. Wes and I agreed that the situation constituted a deterioration and I called the police. It wasn't because of the slap; it was because I had previously bought her some clothes which I then found all cut up. When I asked her why, she couldn't or wouldn't give me an answer. She was hiding things from me, I knew that, but scissors? A blade of some sort? I was worried she'd become a danger to herself. The state of her mental health was a constant concern, but this was a new level of fear.

The police officer was a young lad. He went upstairs, stood outside her room and knocked.

No answer. He introduced himself and asked her to come out.

'Brianna, we just need to know you're okay,' he said.

His voice was soft, mild, very different to the furious shouting that had preceded the 999 call. Wes and I stood on the landing and waited.

'I'm fine,' she said through the door. She was so not fine.

It became clear she wasn't going to open the door and eventually the officer left. Once he'd gone, Brianna went out for a walk. I think it had shaken her, but I couldn't be sure. While she was out, I went into her room. I was shocked by what I saw. Her mirror was smashed to pieces, there were more holes in the walls and what looked like blood stains on her bed and torn up clothes. I stripped and remade her bed and took as much of the rubbish away as I could. It was a quieter Brianna who came home and took herself back up to her room. She didn't acknowledge the clean sheets, but she didn't kick off either. As usual, I went up to bed early. I knocked on her door and opened it a crack, as I had done since the children were tiny.

'Night, Brianna, I love you.'

She looked up at me with vengeful eyes. 'Stop saying that,' she said.

I felt like I had been punched.

'I'm not going to—'

'I mean it. Stop coming into my room every night and saying that.'

'But Brianna, I do love you.'

'I said, STOP SAYING THAT!'

I closed the door behind me, my heart constricting with pain. I couldn't face another battle. Pick your battles, right? Okay, Brianna, I'll stop. It is because of this very sad night that I have since said, whenever asked, never stop telling your children you love them. I guess I'm simply screaming back through time to that moment, to myself: don't listen to her, don't ever stop saying that.

10

Don't Forget the French Fancies

'I don't know how to do all this,' I said to Wes one evening early in the new year.

I had so hoped 2022 would be better, but in the first quarter I had already had to navigate my way through the maze that is getting an ADHD and ASD assessment, and now I needed an EHCP. An Education, Health and Care Plan means the school can get extra funding for a child like Brianna, who had what I and her teachers knew were complex mental health needs and learning difficulties. But our testimony was not enough. So first I headed off in the direction of confirming her Special Educational Needs, a twisting, turning, complex set of corridors which you need to negotiate to get the legal proof required to get a plan. But I hit a dead end because the diagnosis Brianna needed first had not materialized. Although she had taken the Q8 test for ADHD on 23 August 2021, the results seemed impossible to come by. I chased them in November and I chased them again in April. I also organized further assessments for speech and language because Brianna's anxiety was now so intense she refused to go into any classroom or communicate with people for even the few lessons she attended and she found walking the school hallways too much. The school and I spent a lot of time working out ways to accommodate Brianna while giving her a chance to maintain enough attendance hours that she was allowed to stay at school at all. The rest of the time she was at home, on her phone, posting videos and building followers. I chased and chased for the assessment results so many times it began to feel like I was running around in circles; eventually I felt like a mad dog chasing my tail. All the while, I had to keep it together at work and deliver everything that was being asked of me.

On 12 February we all went to Wes's parents' wedding. If you've read anything about Brianna, you've probably seen the photo of her in the pale pink dress with the puffy sleeves that she wore. It hangs in her room. I actually bought five outfits for her to try, because it was impossible to get her to come shopping with me. Her anxiety about how she looked had ballooned into barely leaving the house, so the shopping centre was out of the question. Being in close proximity to me was something she also seemed to loathe. However, there was *no way* I was going to let her go to a wedding in the outfit she wanted to wear. Brianna told me my problem with how she dressed was mine and mine alone. She could wear whatever she wanted, it was the twenty-first century, and I should move with the times. I was told I was a middle-aged freak – it was empowering for women to wear what they liked.

It didn't look empowering to me. I was beginning to think that the filters on her TikTok and Instagram feeds were encouraging her to look more doll-like and gave her strangely elongated limbs. I did not follow her on social media, although I tried. She always blocked me. But I caught glimpses on Alisha's phone and her 'look' made me deeply concerned. Needless to say, I did not look forward to discussing with Brianna what she was going to wear to the family wedding, but it was a discussion I was determined to win. The fuss about leaving the house that day, the tantrums about going at all and the hours of preparation were painful, but, by some miracle, and with a lot of encouragement from Alisha that she did indeed look fabulous, we all went. She did look fabulous. But the more she looked at herself, the less beauty she saw. She thought her fingers were fat. She didn't like her voice. She was in fear of the physical changes that were happening to her that she could not stop. We saw this beautiful young girl in a pretty pink dress; she saw an Adam's apple and hated it. Her confidence was seeping out through her feet.

I thought one-to-one tuition would help her with both addressing her worsening social anxiety and getting her up to speed with maths, English and science so she had a chance of sitting just those basic-requirement GCSEs. Without them, college was not an option. There were funds available to kids who'd fallen behind during Covid, and she had fallen so far behind I thought only tutoring would help. But we needed the assessment review in place first. I hoped things would improve when she attended a weekly social with TAGS. I felt she needed to spend more time with people, real people. It was clear she felt safer with the older kids and the adults in charge, but the few times she did go I noticed an improvement in her general mood. Around Easter she even seemed more positive about going into school and was actually speaking to people there. I was even happier to hear that she had finally begun to connect with the PSHE staff. Normally she pushed the people who were trying to help her away – finally she had made a connection. If she could do that, I hoped there was a chance college would help bring her out of herself and off her phone. I clung on to these moments, but I wasn't naïve. I was resigned to the fact that Brianna would do nothing if she wasn't interested, and the only thing Brianna was remotely interested in, apart from building a massive social media following, was hair and beauty. If she could enrol in a college course early, maybe it would present her with a reason for getting the GCSEs. At two hours for three days a week, she was doing the bare minimum. The school needed her to up that to three hours, but when they did, she would arrive late or leave early to go to the toilets, and the emails from school would once again flood my inbox. We knew what she was doing in the toilets because she was posting the videos she made in there. Getting her interested in anything was always my first challenge; keeping her interested was a whole other battleground. I persevered. But I was punished for it. More and more, Brianna eyed me with hostility.

It felt at times as if I was screaming 'help!' from a burning building but the powers-that-be kept telling me there was no fire. It felt very similar to when, fifteen years earlier, I had been told that the reason I was suffering was because I had postnatal depression and nothing to do with the five years that pre-dated it. It felt the same as being told by the counsellor that because Brianna didn't answer her questions, she could be discharged. Being discharged was the opposite of what she needed. My poor child was suffering so badly. Feeling increasingly stressed about leaving Brianna at home alone, I asked the company that I worked for if I could reduce my hours, or if they would let me go part-time. The work was demanding and needed a full-time employee, so I battled on until March. Meanwhile, life at home was, though hard to imagine possible, getting even more incendiary. I would drive home from work and sit for a while in the car, taking a moment after turning off the ignition and before opening the door. A tiny pause. A momentary sanctuary on wheels before another furious argument erupted.

'I don't know what to do,' I said to Wes, exhausted, dragging my feet on a dog walk after another horrible row.

'It's okay,' he said. 'I've thought it all through. Hand in

your notice, and I'll move in and I'll financially support the family. You can get a part-time job, and then you can be at home to help Brianna and make sure she stays safe.'

God bless that man. So I went for an interview at the nearby Village Hotel and was offered a job as a house-keeping assistant. I worked out my notice and on 19 April I left my corporate life and salary behind and went back to being a cleaner.

'Can we have Domino's tonight?'

This was a nightly request from Brianna and one I des-perately miss hearing. The only time she ate anything close to healthy was when Alisha made dinner. Very rarely did we all sit together, Brianna preferring to take whatever she would eat up to her room. It felt like she couldn't stand the sight of me and couldn't stand to eat the food I had made. I didn't notice when her eating became increasingly selective because, in my mind, it always had been.

As with everything else, I discussed what was happening with the TAF coordinator at school. It was not so difficult to believe Brianna was selectively eating to reduce her body's ability to produce testosterone, because that would stop her muscles from naturally bulking, a sight I know now was beginning to haunt her. She never said anything like that; in fact, she denied there was any sort of problem, insisting that the reason she wasn't eating breakfast was because she felt sick a lot of the time.

My greatest suspicion was that the social media horror show that Brianna was consuming for hours a day was pushing weight loss as entertainment. Ghoulish entertainment, but all the more watchable for it. At first Brianna followed a K-pop influencer, which was reflected in her videos – all cartoon bows and schoolgirl pastels – and when this influencer started to lose weight, Brianna followed suit. I often found out about what Brianna was watching because I could hear it, and when I asked her she would dismiss my concerns, tell me I was a 'stress-head' and that she was only watching 'fashion' tips. I had no idea that the girl she was following claimed to be extolling the virtue of 'healthy' weight loss but was in fact disappearing in front of Brianna's eyes. In the Thinspo, a sickening shorthand for the insidious 'thinspiration' posts, this very ill girl was queen. Her posts were hard to look at, but it was the cruelty and the nonchalance of the comments that made me cry. I truly believe these social media platforms were selling death. To children. This was not a fashion blog, promoting knee-length white socks and micro cheerleader skirts, this was an eating disorder vlog promoting organ failure and death.

I did know Brianna was following a woman who was a former sex worker and now a 'lifestyle' chef. She'd had so much plastic surgery she didn't even look human. Even Alisha tried to warn her sister that this sort of stuff was corrosive, but Brianna wouldn't hear it, or couldn't hear it, even from her beloved sister. Alisha backed off. She knew pressing Brianna on anything was futile and she wanted Brianna to know that, whatever happened, she was there for her whenever Brianna needed her. She learned to wait until Brianna came to her. Neither of us could even knock on her door and ask if she was okay; if we did, something would often be thrown at the door – and if I ever tried to separate her from her phone, things got broken.

How could I give in to what she wanted and leave her alone? I was still her parent and I was still trying to keep her safe, get her to school, encourage her to look after herself and eat well. All the things she hated me doing. There were fireworks and tantrums: shut up, stop talking, go away, not interested, don't talk to me about that! Once again, the link between what she was watching and what I was witnessing was violently denied. I found her running up and down the stairs one day; she told me it was so she didn't put on any weight. But she wasn't gaining weight, she was losing it. And then she started losing her hair. I don't know if she was pulling it out or it was falling out, but a patch of skin appeared behind her left ear. My fear for her wellbeing felt painful.

It was about that point that the school, Brianna and I completed the early help assessment. We were well past early. We were still waiting for the care plan, which had yet to go to the panel that would decide if some extra support could be put in place at school. While we waited, Brianna

was offered support from the council, a Buddy Up programme at a youth club, but she point-blank refused to join
the call that was set up for her. She had also dropped out
of the TAGS sessions and seemed hell bent on becoming
a school refuser. There was no doubt she was utterly miserable and getting worse. When she was asked what was
going well, she said 'nothing'. When she was asked what
she wished for, she said 'nothing'. She said she was tired,
which made sense, as she wasn't eating. But she refused to
acknowledge the link. When a teacher tried to address her
excessive phone use she exploded in their face. We were all
worried about how much time she was spending on her
phone, but she refused, again, to engage with anyone who
mentioned online safety. She would turn on the staff members who were trying valiantly to help her. Every fight left
her more and more isolated.

She got into trouble for silly infringements. Often it
was the length of her nails. She was so proud of herself
for having mastered those nails, but they caused constant
friction at school. Her English teacher sent me work that
Brianna had completed; the teacher was very pleased with
it. It wasn't just a good piece of creative writing, it was a
helpful piece of this complex puzzle.

I look in the mirror, nude acrylic nails longer than the
finger to hide bulkiness. Skin paler than paper with purple
veins peeking through the delicate make-up. Hands and

wrists bony, veiny and stiff. I grab a pink and glittery brush coated with dead hair out of my pink bag with a baby yellow pompom. I brush through my hair, watching it get thinner and thinner. I sigh and blink while my fluttery false eyelashes lightly stroke on my glasses. While putting my brush back into my messy bag filled with rotten out-dated food another girl walks in.

My stomach growls. The feeling of hunger comforts me as I feel the achievement of having an empty stomach. My head dizzy and light. I have never felt better.

I went back to the GP and asked for a referral to CEDS (Community Eating Disorder Services) and CAMHS, since it was clear that we were dealing with a child struggling with so many challenges that surely she was becoming a risk to herself. I was at my wits' end. The school were at their wits' end, and Brianna's suffering intensified. She told her special educational needs coordinator that she did not see the point of living beyond twenty and there was noth-ing she liked about herself. In her writing she said she just wanted to be asleep.

Our first appointment with CEDS didn't come through until 11 July, by which time she was very, very thin. She would hold her arms out to elongate them and stick her tongue out. I didn't know it at the time, but she was mim-icking the preferred pose of a pro-anorexic influencer. At the appointment she was immediately put on an eating plan. My working hours at this point were 6 a.m. till noon, perfect for making appointments in the afternoon, not so good for preparing breakfast. Wes stepped in, and before he went to work he would make Brianna two slices of white toast with butter. Brianna had developed a way of walking through the house as if Wes was not there, but despite being treated appallingly by her, he would take her breakfast up to her room. We never saw her eat it, but there was often an empty plate left on the landing for me to clear up when I got home from work.

Despite sticking to the meal plans and snack times provided by CEDS and the plates of potato waffles, chicken strips and pizza we produced for her, Brianna was still losing weight. She was sent for an appointment at the Whiston Hospital for an ECG because CEDS were worried her restricted calorie intake was damaging her heart. They also took blood so they could keep an eye on her liver function. It was terrifying, but I was told nothing. I don't know what was said in any of those weekly appointments with the eating disorder team because Brianna refused to allow me to go in with her. After one such appointment, the clinic called me, and I thought I was at last going to get some information. But no, it turned out the continued weight loss was not the reason for the call.

'I'm sorry to tell you this, but the last time I took Brianna's blood pressure I noticed cuts on her upper arms.'

'What?'

'I think she's been self-harming.'

'What?'

'She's got cuts on her legs too.'

I felt sick. Surely now everyone would realize my child had serious psychological issues. Surely now the cavalry would arrive.

'I thought you should know.'

And? And nothing. Just letting me know. Weight loss, self-harm, hair loss, body dysmorphia – and there was still no mental health support.

On 1 August I took Brianna to an appointment to discuss medication for the ADHD diagnosis we had waited so long for. The terrible irony was that while she remained under the care of CEDS she could not take the medication that might have helped her get back to full-time education as one of the side effects of ADHD medication was suppressed appetite. She was already noticeably underweight; they wanted her to be nearer 60 kg but she was dropping to the low 50s. By the time we went on our summer holiday to the forest lodge in Crompton, I was on my knees. She looks happy in the videos she and Alisha sent to my mum, but she is so very thin. That's maybe why she was so happy. We had hot tubs and the girls went shopping, we went to Robin Hood's Bay and Whitby Beach, negotiating our way through the summer crowds with our feral dogs, but we had fun. Moments of fun, if I am being totally honest with myself.

One week later I was back at my cleaning job when my mobile rang. It was my mum. She had taken Brianna to her weigh-in appointment that morning. Alarm bells had started ringing before I picked up the call.

'Esther, they want to admit Brianna.'

Panic spread through me. 'What?'

'She's dropped to 48.7 kilos, they are worried about her blood pressure and they took some blood tests. They're worried about her electrolyte levels. I'm taking her to Whiston Hospital.'

'Now?' I burst into tears. 'This is terrible.'

'It's okay, Esther. I think it's the best place for her – they will talk to her, she'll be safe there. She'll get the help she needs. It will be okay.'

'I'm coming.'

'There's no point. I'm with her, she has to check in and they need to find her a bed on the ward. Better you finish work, then go home and get her some things and come later.'

I've never cleaned toilets as fast. This was the worst thing that had happened. Brianna . . . hospitalized, I couldn't get my head around it. I texted her immediately, telling her I would be there as soon as I could, telling her I loved her and how worried I was. Her reply made me cry.

I love you. I was literally so depressed in that meeting and I was trying last week and ate loads. I love you and im sorry xxxxxxxxxxxx

In a daze, I went home and packed her a small bag – the fluffy PJs, of course, a pink hoody, her hormones. She wanted her teeth retainers and the pink container they were stored in; she asked for her pink toothbrush. For once I ignored the revolting state of her room and the fact that I couldn't see the carpet. I had other things to worry about. I texted her and told her I was on my way and how much I loved her.

> B: *Can you bring me some pizza because all the food is horrible lol and I wanna gain waight faster to leave xxxxxxxxxxxxx and snaks.*
> *I love you xxxxxxxxxxxx*
> Me: *I love you too and I want you to get well.*

As soon as I saw her, I knew this was my Brianna: stripped down, sad, afraid and desperately wanting to come home. It was an extraordinary reversal. She hated home, she had said; she hated me; she frequently claimed she wanted to live with my mum, even though after a few hours at my mum's she would storm out in a mood.

'I just want you to get well,' I told her over and over. It wasn't just the calories, it was everything.

Walking back into the house that night without her was a bizarre experience. She was almost always at home. The feeling of her absence was palpable.

> *It's not the same without you at home xxxxxxxxxxx*

It was Wes who found the black bin liner under her bed. It was full of rotting food. The waffles and pizza, the chicken strips and chips. Sometimes she'd thrown the plates in there too. Mouldy cups and encrusted bowls were strewn around the room. And bloody tissues. And cut-up clothes. Her mirror was smashed. It was like walking into a messed-up mind. I went to sleep less terrified, knowing she would be watched throughout the night. When I woke up there were reams of texts from Brianna. She had her phone, but with no Wi-Fi and therefore no internet, all she could do was play *Crossy Road* and send texts. So she sent texts. Many, many precious texts.

Im excited to be home next week already lol xxxxxxxx
They kept doing my blood pressure in my sleep lol
They tried to do it in my sleep lol xxxxxxxxxxxxx
But I woke up every time
MY PHONE CHARGER!!
Bring me a mars bar to pls lol xxxxxxxxxxxxxx
See you after work. Lol. Member my French fancys pls.
Porige and tost.
Some lady sat with me for half an hour watching me eat
it lol xxxxxxxx

They were supposed to sit with her for an hour. I told her I would be having a word! But Brianna said they seemed busy and understaffed, so I didn't. The healthcare assistant was lovely and after a while the two of them started to chat a bit, but really her job was to sit and watch Brianna eat. Every morsel of food that passed her lips was measured and recorded. Even after she had a snack, the door would be left open for an hour so there was no chance she could go to the bathroom and be sick. And there were regular snacks between meals and before bed. Brianna wasn't a risk: she ate everything; my little homebody didn't play up because she wanted to come home. She missed the dogs, she missed Domino's pizza, she missed me. She was offered a wheelchair if she wanted to go outside, but she refused. Since she was not under any circumstances allowed to walk anywhere, Brianna stayed in her room.

> *Just ordered my lunch xxxxxxxxxx*
> *Dinner lady was nice.*

I dropped in every day, sometimes with Mum and Alisha, often on my own. With nothing else to occupy her, sometimes her texting got a fraction demanding. Especially if I didn't respond immediately.

> 20.21 *Call me.*
> 20.22 *Call me again.*
> 20.32 *Call me.*
> 20.34 *Ugh fine whatevah*

Another time I'd been driving so couldn't respond to her and she got immediately resentful about my phone's automatic reply. However, when I explained, she would follow it up with a laughing emoji. It felt less precarious, less brittle than before, and I really hoped she had scared herself and we had turned a corner. Other times she got crotchety when we visited. She would long for us to come but then tell us to go. Once she hid in the toilet when I came; she couldn't explain why and she said sorry. Apologies were rare so I took them as progress too. When she was rude to me, she explained by text that it was only because she was depressed. Other times she would simply interrupt a conversation between me, her and Alisha and say abruptly, 'You can go now.'

'We're not leaving yet, Brianna.'

'I want you to go.'

If it looked like it was going to escalate, we would make a quick exit. But we tried to get her chatting about something she was interested in, and if we succeeded, the moment would pass. She was so childlike, never more than when she was devoid of make-up, in that hospital bed, in her pyjamas.

I asked the staff a lot of questions about why she'd lost so much weight and how and what we should do, and was there anything I should know, but it wasn't an acute eating disorder ward, and she was eating and putting on weight so they just seemed pleased. I was pleased too. At no point did anyone ask me or warn me about pro-anorexic content online; they did not mention 'famous' anorexic influencers. I was later told they did not mention it to the kids who came through their clinic because they didn't want to advertise the fact that such content was out there. But any child who searched up weight loss would find out within seconds who was 'successfully' losing weight – regardless of how healthy it was – and now that the multimillion-dollar tech company had grabbed their attention, its highly effective engagement model was trained specifically at them to keep it. In Brianna's case, unbeknownst to me, her attention was being kept by a woman so close to death she looked like a skeleton. But that skeleton had millions of followers. And thanks to the algorithm, now she had one more. My child.

Without Wi-Fi, Brianna had one week without any negative influence at all, and the difference was extraordinary.

The nurse who sits with me is dead funny lol
She said she goes the strip club when playing GTA
haha xxxxxxxxxxx
Love you xxxxxxxxxxxx
Feel lonely now lolz xxxxxxxxxxxxxxxxxx
Playing Crossy Rd.

This terrible thing that I had been so distraught about had turned into something unimaginable. A precious week of laughing emojis and I love yous and xxxxxxx and a bit of light-hearted banter. I told her I missed her, that I was looking forward to seeing her; she told me she loved me, she missed us and wanted to come home. By Monday 22nd we were discussing getting her new shoes for school, which in my world was hopeful. She really wanted to come home, but the eating disorder team told her it would be another week until her bloods had levelled. They told her if she carried on eating everything, she might be allowed to come home for tea on Thursday for a home visit. Bless her, she ate everything they put in front of her. Weetabix, pasta, tea and Digestives, yogurt, more pasta, gingernuts, more pasta, and slowly the scales went up, so she was allowed to come home for tea.

I'll have a bath on Thursday and tidy my room.

Music to my ears!
'I'll help you,' I replied.
Help me have a bath . . . Laughing emojis.
Although she was now eating well, she still wasn't looking after herself in other ways, and her personal hygiene continued to be a problem.
'Come on, clean your teeth.'
'Come on, out of bed, time for a shower.'
It was like having a small child again. With no one to perform for on social media, she didn't bother washing or putting on make-up or doing her hair, or anything. Her bed was messy and her pillow would often be on the floor when I came in. Not good for my self-diagnosed clean freakery, so I would get her in the shower then make her bed all straight – I probably should have been a nurse; I do like a hospital corner – and then I would put her back into bed

in her clean pyjamas with her pillows all fluffed up around her head. It was a joy to care for her – it had been a long time since she had let me.

'Let's make it nice and tidy so you're all straight and comfortable.' I tucked her in like I had when she was a child, because that is what she was, just a child, lying in bed, tucked in, no make-up, no wig, no edge or attitude, just my precious baby who wanted to come home. She let me lie alongside her, kiss her forehead and give her a hug. With no access to Wi-Fi to draw her away, this terrible frightening time, when I thought the worst had happened, was in fact a very precious ten days. After all the misery and shouting, I got my lovely, loving, funny child back. Her essential self. I couldn't wait to get her home. Six months later I would see my child tucked up lifeless under a duvet, again with no make-up, no wig, no edge or attitude, just my precious baby, and I knew as if she'd sat up and told me herself, all she wanted was to come home. Remembering her like that is torture. But forgetting her is worse.

11

Leave Me Alone /
Don't Leave Me Alone

I'm starting to run out of things to watch . . . any recommendations?

It was an innocuous request in May 2020 on Instagram. The then twelve-year-old said her favourite film was *Sweeney Todd*, so people on Insta helpfully suggested true-crime documentaries to watch, which she did. She started watching documentaries about serial killers, homing in on Jeffrey Dahmer and the English doctor Harold Shipman. But it was the Night Stalker, Richard Ramirez, who she really admired. Knowing so much about him, she could quote him and boasted she could talk about him for over two hours. That investigation and research would have taken a lot of time. If a child is consuming that much information on serial killers, someone or something should have noticed and intervened. I think something did notice, an engagement-driven algorithm designed to send the person browsing more of what they were interested in, and that intervention pulled her further in rather than pulling her out. By the time she was fifteen she was no longer watching true crime, she was watching real crime. At home she was quiet, at school she was polite, but in her head and on her phone she was thinking about and viewing real violence against real people, including unspeakable torture, rape, snuff videos and murder. In August she first offered to help her good friend kill a boy who was getting too close to a girl he was infatuated with.

Just ask me to and I will

A cursory search of her phone would have found many messages on WhatsApp and Snapchat discussing it, including cutting out his heart, cooking it and eating it. She also shared videos of killing and torture with him and an advert for an underground site offering live footage of everything she was looking for. How? She had downloaded an app known as an onion router on to her home screen, which, by going through encrypted layers, gave the fifteen-year-old access to illegal content on the Dark Web.

I love watching torture vids
Real ones on dark web
Im just happy ive found a good red room

I don't know if using a service like SafetyNet to screen for danger words or illegal apps would have stopped her from wanting to kill another human being, but it might have stopped her from succeeding. Her growing and unchecked fantasies of hurting another person led her to take edible cannabis gummies into school. On 28 September 2022 she shared the edibles with a thirteen-year-old, who took them and became very ill. The police were called, but the parents chose not to take the case further, as intention to harm was hard to prove. She was suspended from her school, Culcheth High School, for five days. That wasn't the end of it, however, because the girl had previously broken the rules about drugs and had been suspended before, so a managed transfer was suggested. This would put her on a trial placement at another school to avoid permanent expulsion. Birchwood was contacted.

Meanwhile, Brianna had started a new term at Birchwood that same September. While she was in hospital we had excitedly bought new shoes and new clothes for her. She had missed her SEN coordinator, who she was close to, and had a meeting planned with her the day after she'd been discharged. I emailed the school to let them know what had happened and the eating plan that Brianna would have to be on when she returned. It was a good meeting. The SEN coordinator and Brianna discussed her going back to school for longer hours, and even attending some of the classes that had fewer pupils. Brianna was excited about returning to Textiles, a subject she had taken up during the previous term and had been doing well in. This was a breakthrough and would not have been possible without the profound support from the school. But I was nervous.

She had been so excited about leaving hospital she had started getting ready to leave the ward at 8.15 in the morning. Hair, make-up, clean clothes – the full Brianna. It was good to see her taking pride in her appearance; it was good to know she was happy to be coming home. I picked her up and drove back to Warrington. And then there is a blank in my memory. I think this is because I don't want to remember what happened next. She was happy to see the dogs. She was happy we were getting pizza. But as soon as it arrived, she took hers and disappeared upstairs to her room. If I had hoped things would be different, I was sadly mistaken. The door closed. She was back on her phone. Within seconds, we'd lost her again.

During only the second week of term, things began to slide.

Brianna said she did not want to attend even the smaller classes today. She wasn't in a great mood. She asked to go to the toilet; I asked a TA to take her as it is school policy for students to be escorted to the toilet (students in classrooms need to be escorted by whoever is on call). Brianna did not like this idea and sat down again. She then picked up her bag and walked off – she didn't come back to the inclusion room and signed herself out.

Here we go again, I thought, reading the email. I was exhausted by the prospect of it all. I tried to talk to her. I kept asking her what I could do to help. But it was like talking to a scowling brick wall. I knew she felt her phone was her friend, surgically attached to her hand, but I hated it. The downward slide picked up speed – it was a vertiginous descent back to square one. Selective eating. Poor hygiene. Filthy room. School refusal and a contemptuous hatred of me when I asked her about any of it. I wanted to take her phone off her forever. I wish I had, but I knew even that was futile, and possibly more dangerous. She was terrible with her phone, but I was terrified about what would happen if I took this one 'joy' away from her. She was at risk from the online world with it; she was at risk from herself and acute isolation without it. One day, I honestly believe we will look back at this time and wonder how on earth we let these gigantic tech companies play with our children's lives. Unless, of course, we do nothing about it, and then we will look back at this time with nostalgia.

Brianna's only other source of joy was messing around with her sister. It usually involved the phone as well, such was her addiction. But at least I have those moments to revisit. They would go for walks, sometimes – though rarely – without the full make-up and hair, just Bree and Alisha, off to the shops for a chocolate bar and a drink to have in the park. One time Brianna found a kid's scooter and took it for a ride. Another time she fed a dying bee honey and water. In the face of all her hostility, I clung to these moments to keep me going. I had to keep going for her sake, keep trying to find a way through to her, because I really did fear I might lose her.

I had one weapon left against the monster in her hand. The PIN code. One day after a row about being in trouble at school for making TikTok videos in the toilets when she should have been in lessons, I confiscated the bloody thing. She went nuts. I gave the phone to Wes, who took it into my room, locked the door so Brianna couldn't get in and went through it. I had done this since the kids had first been given phones; it wasn't a new thing, it had just become a more incendiary thing. Previously I hadn't found anything to be really worried about, but I now know she was probably hiding stuff behind false app icons that I would not have known to look at. What we discovered that day was different. Brianna was on Twitter. Now called X. It wasn't politics or news she was looking at. It was porn. I didn't even know this was allowed on social media. That was terrifying, but it was the unending messages from men that really turned my blood cold. Wes scrolled through them, deleting and blocking everything he could find. He put back every parental control he knew about, reset the PIN so she couldn't change it and, eventually, reluctantly, handed her back the phone. She would not talk to me about any of it and in fact ceased to communicate with me at all. I was at a total loss. Somehow I had to find another way.

*

The head of Birchwood, Emma Mills, met the pupil from Culcheth and her mother to discuss the managed transfer. It was clear that the girl came from a loving and supportive family. Both women understood the perils of being a teenager, but in this case the incident with the cannabis gummy felt like nothing more than a misdemeanour, and no one had mentioned spiking or lacing or tricking. The other young person said she didn't know what she'd taken, but it was one word against another and it wasn't beyond any teacher's imagination that a schoolkid might lie if they got caught breaking the rules. Sitting upright and speaking quietly, the pupil told the head of Birchwood that she'd learned her lesson, she understood the new school rules. She said she was ready for her second chance.

I thought college was Brianna's last chance – and my only hope. Maybe it was mad to think that my child who barely left her room would be able to go to college the following academic year, but it was worth a try. With the school's encouragement, I applied to Warrington and Vale Royal College for Brianna to study Level 2 Beauty Therapy. Her SEN coordinator explained she would need to meet their requirements of getting two or more GCSEs if she wanted to go. Brianna still had an okay relationship with her at the time and in their weekly meetings said she was keen to try. At one point I was told by the school she wanted to sit her Chemistry GCSE mock, even though she knew she might not be able to answer much. She needed to get to school early to sit it, and I was sent an email asking me to help her get there on time. I was beginning to get a little impatient: did they really think, after all I had told them, that I could get Brianna to do anything? At all? In fact, I would say the opposite was true. I was leaving the house at 7 a.m. to get to work.

I had been contacted by my old colleague and told there was a part-time job going at the food company I used to work at. Was I interested? I absolutely was. It was better paid, I could still get Brianna to her appointments, and it gave me a moment when I could do something other than worry about her.

There was so much to worry about. On a weigh-in and blood-test appointment at Whiston Hospital, Brianna had managed to drop her phone from the raised walkway that took us from the car park to the hospital. It smashed beyond repair. There had been many times when I had wanted to smash the phone myself, but Brianna was dependent on it and, though I knew she was addicted, when she asked for a new phone for her sixteenth birthday at the start of November, I did not have the nerve to say no. I bought the phone and ordered a beautiful pink two-tier cake that looked like stacked wrapped parcels complete with a polka-dot bow. She unwrapped the phone, and when I told her we could set it up together she announced that because she was now sixteen I was allowed no access to her phone at all. She would not let me look at it, there would be no parental controls and she never had to tell me her passcode.

With no boundaries, she sunk deeper and deeper into harmful content that caught her and trapped her. As prey, she was perfect – it was like she'd been dangling in this giant, dark, dangerous matrix, a target for all the harmful content on the Web. The impact on her was visible, palpable and terrifyingly fast. Support was something we both needed but something Brianna wouldn't accept, and I couldn't locate. That's not strictly true: I could locate it, but it didn't seem to make a difference. We'd been through Early Help, St Joseph's, CAMHS, an EHCP (an Education, Health and Care Plan, which refused the extra funding) and CEDS, the eating disorder clinic, but she was still underweight, self-harming, putting herself at risk online.

I still had to get her blood-tested for hormones, stay on top of her asthma medication, pay and order the trans meds, get her to her CEDS appointments, the ECG appointments, monitor her calorie intake, take her to see a nutritionist, monitor and pay for the hormone treatment appointments, review the ADHD medication, attend TAF meetings, complete the EHCP annual review, make sure she attended at least two hours of school most days and, since she had turned sixteen, I now had to add getting her Personal Independence Payments organized and get her back into CAMHS. All in the face of abject resistance and hostility. But still the thing that worried me most was the fact that with only two supervised hours a day three days a week at school, she was so often home alone with her phone. I had no idea who she might let in, I had no idea who she was talking to or what she was putting out online for anyone to see. She was a danger to herself, she was a danger to Alisha, and I was terrified all the time. On 16 November her Autistic Spectrum Disorder diagnosis was confirmed – just in the nick of time, I thought. This would surely be the thing that unlocked the help I so desperately needed. I had lost control and was absolutely shattered.

On 30 November we received a voicemail from Brianna's head of year about a member of the public raising concerns about Brianna's social media content. When I asked what the concerns were, they would not say. I could not sleep for worrying and in the morning decided I had no choice but to contact social services. I called MASH (the Multi-Agency Safety Hub), which coordinates an urgent response when a child or adult is considered a risk to themselves. It involves the police, social workers, the NHS and the council. I rang the number until it rang off. As a last resort, I asked Brianna if I could check her phone. I tried to tell her that our relationship would be better if she let me check it, take it overnight as I used to. Then at least I would know she was sleeping properly. The answer was no.

I couldn't sleep and in the middle of the night I got up to go to the toilet. I saw the light on under Brianna's door. She would often fall asleep with the lights on, so I decided to creep in and turn it off. I turned the handle and pushed . . .

'Go away!' Brianna pushed back. I couldn't open the door because she was behind it. I could tell from the light that she was on the phone.

'What are you doing on your phone? It's the middle of the night.'

'Leave me alone!!'

Go away. Leave me alone. Go away. Leave me alone.

Fearful and sad, there was no way I could sleep now. Eventually I got up and wrote everything down in a long email to our TAF contact explaining exactly how I felt. This was the top line.

I have lost control. I don't know what she's doing online. I am worried about the safety of my other child and what Brianna might bring to the family home. I am really concerned that I will arrive home from work one day and Brianna will be raped or murdered.

Those are the very words I wrote. That is how desperate I was. I wasn't embellishing for effect, I was drowning.

It is incredibly sad to me that, in the same month, Brianna got an offer for the beauty therapy course. Although they only required two GCSEs, they did need a 75 per cent attendance rate. Brianna was on 28.5 per cent. No one thought she could turn that around, because as we headed through December her behaviour was getting even more erratic. She did a U-turn on going into lessons and was back in the inclusion unit, and often not even there. The council-led initiative to provide education, training, work or volunteering for sixteen- to nineteen-year-olds started to look at options for Brianna; no one wants kids to just drop off the map. There was a place for extremely disruptive children, but we all agreed Brianna would not fare well there. When asked what she was interested in, she replied, 'I don't care.' What was working well?

Nothing.

Don't speak to me.

I cannot stand speaking to people.

I just want to be on my own.

I don't care about anything.

Even her TikTok videos took on a grungy, messy vibe. Gone were the immaculately ironed locks, the puckered lips and pretty pastels. Less vibrant and vital, she had dropped back to 51 kilos. I think she was lonely and sad, and the pressure of keeping up her TikTok persona was exhausting her. I think her phone, the place that she had once gone to for community, comfort and affirmation, was crippling her.

It was at around this point that I recall feeling like I could do no more. I could not fight her addiction to the phone. I couldn't take the abuse. And with an ASD diagnosis, perhaps I had permission to surrender. Maybe I should have known she was autistic for years: her inability to read social cues or see potential danger, her abruptness and struggle to understand other people's views and feelings, her manic obsessions with some things and her equally pathological disinterest in others. If I had known, maybe things would have turned out differently. This is why I feel like I let her down, and it crucifies me. I have to tell myself I couldn't have stopped a pandemic. I couldn't have foreseen that locking down children like that was a short-term win for them but a long-term loss for their development. I couldn't have known about the built-in addiction of social media. But nevertheless, I regret every single time I got cross with her behaviour, and I am so, so very sorry. Finally, though, I just stopped nagging her and tried to keep out of her way, thinking perhaps then at least we would have some peace at home.

'I like your eyeliner.'

'Thanks,' said Brianna.

Make-up – a way to her heart. It was 11 December when Brianna crossed paths with the girl who was beginning her managed transfer to Birchwood. The school couldn't accommodate all her subjects so occasionally she, too, was doing catch-up work in the inclusion room. Brianna should have been back in the classroom by then, but being in the classroom meant putting away her phone, which she simply refused to do, to the point that the school had no choice but to administer a suspension. When she turned up at home unannounced, taking a leaf out of my grandfather's book, I made her stay out.

On 15 December the new girl at Birchwood sent her friend from her old school another text message:

I'm obsessed over someone I know but I don't have feelings for them. She's called Brianna. I don't know how to explain.

The new girl suggested to Brianna that they go to McDonald's after school. Brianna said yes. Needless to say, I was pleased, because Brianna had retreated from all of us, even Alisha. I knew she'd been posting videos of herself with blood running from her wrist. The cut itself was hidden, or amplified, by a smiling Hello Kitty digital sticker. Was this a clamour for attention or a cry for help? And in the world of social media, are the two the same?

I never got anywhere near her phone, so I genuinely had no idea who she was contacting, but one evening in late December, very unusually, Brianna got in the shower and left her phone on the landing. I noticed it because I went to get the Christmas wrapping paper which I kept just behind the bookcase on the landing. I couldn't unlock the phone because I didn't know her PIN code, but Snapchat notifications were constantly pinging on to her home screen. I took a glimpse. The number of messages coming in was terrifying. I scrolled through so many profile emojis of men. She was being notified of these messages every second. As was Twitter. And Wink. And Wizz. And Face-time. And BIGO Live, a live-streaming app that at a glance looks child-friendly with its cartoon dinosaur logo but in fact lets you chat with the 'hottest' girls from 150 countries. Quietly, my hand shaking, I took a video. This was surely the proof I needed that she was in grave danger. The ASD diagnosis meant she was not able to keep herself safe. What did stranger danger look like in the twenty-first century? It looked like a Snapchat notification.

For a moment on Christmas morning, it was like I had my excitable, funny kid home. She came bounding down the stairs for breakfast and presents, chatting happily and making us laugh with her usual acerbic humour. But it was fleeting, and as soon as she'd got her gifts she was back upstairs and she would not leave her room again. No amount of pleading and begging from me or Alisha could get her to change her mind. So we went to my mum's for dinner without her. She spent her last Christmas alone. Well, not alone. But not surrounded by the people who loved and cared for her.

The New Year brought new suspensions. We had a meeting at school, but by this time I'd gone a bit quiet. I wasn't sure what more I could say. Brianna removed herself from the meeting because she couldn't be bothered to participate in anything, and when we went to update her, the social worker introduced herself to Brianna and tried hard to explain to her the seriousness of being excluded from school. Brianna just looked through her while tracing her pink fluffy pen over her face with petulant disinterest. She wasn't speaking to me. Instead, from yards away, she informed me by text to go home, she was going out with her new friend. Fine. Good. The fight had gone out of me. I was glad she had a friend.

Later in January, we managed to have a lovely few days back at the forest holiday park for Wes's birthday. Meanwhile, a lad I did not know narrowly escaped death when Brianna's new friend, together with her old schoolfriend from Culcheth High School, tried, unsuccessfully, to lure him to Linear Park using a fake Instagram account. The two of them had discussed ways to kill this lad, with the schoolfriend suggesting he could be beaten to death, or that they could build a noose and make it look like suicide. But Brianna's new friend had other ideas.

Nah just stab him, slit his throat and stab his back.

She knew a hidden spot. They would meet up by the wooden posts in Linear Park . . . you can probably guess the rest of the plan. Luckily for their intended victim, he got suspicious and blocked her on Instagram. She was not deterred.

If we can't get him we can get Brianna tomorrow. She's back from holiday.

And she was. My mum had come to pick Alisha and Brianna up and take them home for school on Monday. Wes and I stayed another night. There are moments that, however hard I try, my brain drags me back to. And one of those is that weekend in the forest lodge. Brianna and I sat in the hot tub together. I asked her if she was okay.

'I feel really sad.'

Brianna never talked about her feelings, only things.

'Like there isn't any point.'

It was the same chilling despondency she'd talked about in the Early Help annual review, and it frightened me. I wish I had sat there with her, acknowledged how miserable she was feeling, but I panicked and shifted into fix-it mode. If you would just go outside, be with people, get some sleep . . . those fundamentally important things you need to do to counter low mood and depression and everything your phone is stopping you from . . .

'You will never know how I feel!'

We did not get to the end of the conversation. We barely started. Brianna got out of the hot tub and furiously walked away. Come back, I'm sorry, let's talk about how you feel and what you're sad about. But she can't, and I have to live with that. Sometimes when I am doing interviews I hear her in my head: she was right, I could not and cannot know how she felt, and that is why I try, I really try, to talk about my experience, not hers.

'Hi Bree, I'm home!' I shouted up the stairs, then went straight to the kitchen to start making tea.

It was just after 6 p.m. on 23 January when I heard what I thought was Brianna screaming. The noise came again. I ran out of the kitchen, thinking: this time, she's done it, she's cut herself so deeply that I won't be able to save her. I pelted up the stairs, bursting into her room, expecting the worst. She was on her bed, clutching her stomach, rolling around in agony. I ran to her. No blood. She was screaming in pain; I'd never seen her like that. She'd never been a sickly child, quite the opposite in fact: she seemed indestructible. It was frightening.

'Where's the pain?' I thought it might be appendicitis.

'I think I'm dying.'

I stood up to run and get my phone.

'Don't leave me,' she pleaded.

I didn't want to, but I needed my phone to look up the symptoms.

'I need to get help.'

'Please, don't leave me. Mum, I think I'm going to die.'

I put my hand on her.

'I'll be straight back,' I promised her, and ran downstairs.

As I grabbed my phone, I heard a loud splash. I ran back upstairs, and Brianna was hanging off the side of her bed, sick all over the floor. The vomit was like clear water with grape skins in it. Maybe she'd binged on grapes and her stomach couldn't cope after starving herself for so long. I cleaned up the mess and, although there was a little immediate relief, she was still writhing around and visibly uncomfortable. I thought about calling 999, but by the time I'd finished cleaning up the pain had subsided. She pulled her knees up to her chest, but I could see the intense pain had left her face. She started breathing more calmly. I tucked her in. Not appendicitis or a tummy bug. It must have been something she'd eaten, but I couldn't think what that might have been.

> Girl: *I am still trying to kill her and the easiest way is pill overdose ppl already know shes depressed and shit so nobody would get suss but for some reason she has a high tolerance*
> Girl: *Like I gave her some today that shld have been enough to kill her but she didn't die.*
> Boy: *Try doubling the dose what if you added it to a drink*
> Boy: *What about in a maccies milkshake.*
> Girl: *Brianna is still ill. Those tablets I gave her might slowly be killing her.*

It is absolutely true that if Brianna had died that day from a pill overdose we would all have thought it was another tragic case of a young person ending their life by suicide. In 2023, 6,069 people in England and Wales succeeded. In a notebook in her room she'd written that she couldn't see herself living beyond her teens. We would have found it that day, or the next, and it would have confirmed our fears. Brianna's erroneous death certificate would have made it 6,070, one more sad statistic which we would have had to learn to live with. Or maybe she wouldn't have been sick and we would have had to take her to hospital . . . Would she have had her stomach pumped? Would it have been discovered that the 'grape skins' were in fact the jelly shells of the Rapid Ibuprofen that she and her new friend had taken. Or would Brianna have insisted she did not take them knowingly? Would we have believed her? Would she have been put on suicide watch? Would she have told us who had given them to her, or who had tricked her into taking them, and how do you trick someone into taking ibuprofen in that quantity unless you think you're taking something else, something you think will make you high . . .

After Brianna died, I met a friend of hers from Scotland who Brianna had made online, who she told a lot to and yet had never met in person. She had told this friend she thought she was trying MDMA that day, but after she was so ill the two of them had discussed the possibility that the new friend was trying to poison Brianna and perhaps she wasn't such a good friend, perhaps she'd been befriending her with ulterior motives, perhaps there was a transphobic ingredient to this. If only I had known!

Stop! This sort of thinking is what takes me to a very dark place. Stand up. Feet to the floor. Outside, I breathe deep inhalations of cool air. Look up. I notice the light on the leaves. The arms of a tree stretching out its branches as if offering me a hug. I stand a while in nature's embrace and clear my mind. Later I will walk. I will go to bed early and sleep. I will make myself do what I could not make my child do. I will stave off the depressive thoughts with exercise, meditation and sleep. Some days I will find that is possible. Others it will take every last ounce of energy I have not to succumb.

If Brianna had really thought her new friend had purposely tried to hurt her, I don't think she would have met up with her again. Yet four days later the two of them went to Asda to buy hair dye. When I say 'buy', I am not certain anything was being paid for. Brianna sent me a picture of her dyeing her friend's hair red in the public toilets nearby. She told me this girl was a bit too 'Emo' for her liking and not really her style. So what was the draw? I knew Brianna was curious about drugs; she had talked about taking coke, claiming it was a glamorous drug, a skinny girl's drug. I had been so clear with my children that there was nothing glamorous about drugs. I had told them of the terrible mistakes I had made, how many lives drugs ruined. But Brianna had found a willing partner in crime. Someone who claimed, at least, that she could get her hands on some cocaine.

*

On 28 January, Brianna's new friend met her old school-friend from Culcheth High School, the boy who had eagerly discussed killing a lad who had shown interest in a girl he liked, in Linear Park. He brought the thirteen-inch hunting knife with a five-inch blade that he had bought on a ski trip that Christmas in Bulgaria for £13.50. He'd proudly posted a picture of it on a WhatsApp group, along with all the other shiny, metallic weapons that had taken his fancy. It was sharp enough to cut his skin, he assured her, when she asked him if it would definitely 100 per cent kill my child. They had decided to stick to the plan they had made for their first intended victim: Linear Park, remote spot, use the knife. But Brianna didn't show.

Im fucking pissed Brianna just last minute said she cant come coz of her stepdads birthday dinner . . . she said she might be able to past 5.

This wasn't true. Brianna had lied to get out of going. That was quite like Brianna, to make friends then move on, and this occasion was no different. She was fast going off this girl, but sadly not fast enough. The friend was persistent, though, determined to find a way to fulfil her desire to kill and knew exactly what to use to tempt Brianna out.

We could give her an od of coke, she suggested, but quickly changed her mind.

Nah, lets just stab her. Its more fun.

Not that I knew any of this at the time, but luring Brianna out with the promise of taking cocaine was the plan.

On 3 February their plan nearly worked. Wes and I had gone out to celebrate my new position as a full-time Senior New Product Development Technologist at my old workplace. It really was my dream job and I was over the moon. Brianna texted me just before we were going to sleep. She had decided to go out after school to McDonald's which had been fine by me, but now she wanted to stay out a bit later with her new friend. I may have given up nagging her about her room, her appearance and her attitude, but her safety was not up for negotiation. There was no way I was going to let her stay out after 9 p.m., even on a Friday night, no matter the pushback from her. We had a fairly furious text exchange, but finally I got her to agree to come home. And, thankfully, she did.

Four days later my mum went to the school to try and find a way through to Brianna, as her attendance was so low and erratic they had no option but to permanently exclude her. It didn't work. Brianna was rude, disengaged, rolled her eyes and said she was done with school. My mum thanked them for all they had done and then, feeling as resigned and dejected about Brianna's educational prospects as I did, left.

I have a few things to be eternally grateful for, and one of them is that I managed to get Brianna to come home that night. I am amazed I did, such was her belligerent mood at the time. I believe they planned to kill her that night. The girl had tried to get her male friend and accomplice out on a previous evening, but it was a school night, so he couldn't come. Friday the 3rd was the next date they'd agreed on. There would have been no dog-walkers out at 9 p.m. on a cold February night that far from the gates of Linear Park. If they had succeeded, she might have been left alone in that dark wood and none of us would have known where she was or what had happened to her, for hours, maybe years, maybe ever. I know Brianna was not alone at the end, and that brings me a little comfort. I am grateful for small things, but that, for me, is huge.

12

I Knew This Would Happen

And it is agony. The rest is a blur.

13

Under a Pink Sky

I pick up a photograph and draw Brianna into the space where she should be. And suddenly she is there, she's back, right here with me. I am so relieved I wake up. The house is deathly quiet. She isn't here, but she isn't quite gone either. I am trying to find her in my sleep, and when I wake my body tries to fight the truth. I stumble into her room and sit on the floor. The filthy floor I had nagged her about. Why? What did it matter now? The thought of all those arguments makes me feel sick. The agony rips through me and there are moments when I feel I can't contain the pain.

'Where are you, Brianna?' I sob. 'Where are you?' For the briefest of moments, I expect her to reply. Pull a face, stick out her tongue, make a noise. Nothing. Outside, the sky starts to turn a soft pink. My eyes bulge out of my swollen face; for three days I have not stopped crying. Though Wes has tried to feed us, I haven't eaten for a week. The grief is moving around my body like a virus which my immune system tries to suppress. It is losing, and I start swelling up in strange places. My right arm seems to be the worst. It looks distended, like it might burst. I don't want to tell anyone what has happened because it can't be happening. The police liaison officer comes. They have a lot of questions and after what feels like hours, Wes bundles Alisha and me into the car and we drive to Lymm Dam, where Brianna once heard ducks screaming.

I am terrified by the thought of seeing someone we know. I can't face that. No one knows what to say, and all I can say is this shouldn't be happening, this shouldn't be happening. Wes parks in a small layby just next to the canal. It is late afternoon when we get out of the car.

'Look!' I exclaim, pointing up. The sky is covered in a thick, undulating pink duvet. It is heartbreakingly beautiful. The slow-flowing canal looks like a strip of pink. Alisha, Wes and I hold each other a little closer.

'She's here,' I say. 'I can feel her.' How did I know it was her? I really don't like the colour pink – I used to try my best to get her to wear anything other than pink – but pink was not just a colour to her, it was a way of life. So of course, as with anything to do with my extremely determined child, she *would* paint the sky pink, and not just any pink, a French Fancy pink, just to remind me who was still queen.

My phone buzzes to tell me that somebody is at my house, ringing my doorbell. It is my oldest friend, Vicky. Auntie Vicky. My friend has become my family. But I can't speak to her over a doorbell app. We walk on. Ten minutes later the doorbell rings again. Vicky is back. I put my phone away. If I don't, I will look at the last message I sent Brianna. The one where I told her how proud I was that she had got herself on the bus. There is only one tick, so I fear she never read it. We walk very slowly, noticing the fresh, vivid green shoots of new snowdrops just beginning to emerge from the dark ground. One or two already have flowers, bright white bells, bowing at us. I know why they move me so much – just noticing them fully has given me a little break from the pain and, for the briefest of moments, we are okay. If this is possible, then I know we will be okay again. Under the pink sky and with flowers at our feet, we wander back to the car.

Vicky was sitting on the doorstep. She grabbed hold of me and Alisha, and we hugged and cried. We didn't speak because there were no words. Wes parked the car and followed us in.

'Sorry for your loss,' a man shouted from over the road. Wes closed the door, cocooning us in our crippling grief. From that moment to now, Vicky has been stalwart in her support of us. We were shattered into a million pieces by Brianna's murder and we had a long, long way to go before we could even start to put ourselves back together, but I do think on that very first day Vicky picked up the most important piece, the piece that said, while grief is lonely, you are not alone. Alisha's friends came next. I was so thankful that they were there. She is blessed with a wonderful group of friends. We talked about Brianna a lot, but we kept the speculation and suspicions of what had happened to her out of the house. If people were talking about it, they were advised not to do it in my earshot. Mostly we just wept together because, honestly, what could anyone say? The doorbell started to ring more often; it was either flowers or friends. Flowers from friends, and then just flowers. During the first week the cards started to arrive. Sometimes they were simply addressed to Brianna's family, Warrington, but they found us all the same. Every time the doorbell rang, I had two thoughts running concurrently.

This should not be happening. We are not alone.

Brianna was the extrovert, the attention-grabber. Alisha, I and Wes are not, so the media coverage of the murder, at first, was extremely hard to fathom. But I was thankful too, because the newsreaders could deliver the words I could not utter. At least I was spared that. I knew from my own mindfulness practice that news needs to be digested in small amounts and, sometimes, not at all. During Covid I found myself slumping whenever I listened to the news, so I stopped. For eight years I had kept up a routine to keep myself sane. I woke up and did a ten-minute meditation, and in the evening I would light a candle, do some stretches and meditate again. Focusing on what I was grateful for that day was something I did both purposefully through meditation and periodically throughout the day. A robin. A good sandwich. A fresh brew. I had trained my brain to notice these small things to stop me from internally spiralling into intrusive thoughts. After Brianna's murder, I stopped watching the news again, and my every waking minute was about clinging on to those tiny moments and slivers of thanks for what I still had, rather than being sunk by the weight of what we had lost.

So yes, I was grateful that I didn't have to tell people what had happened. I never have had to, but I have had to listen to presenters telling me what happened, and I will never, ever get used to that. During those first hours and days, people would hug me and tell me how sorry they were and I would think, why are you sorry? You didn't kill my child. I think back now and realize, though I was on my feet, I wasn't functioning. A lot of it is muffled and distorted. It felt like days passed before I became aware of the role Brianna's new friend had played, but it was only hours. It felt like weeks passed before I spoke to a funeral director, but it was days. I felt like it was months before I was picking a casket and ordering a hearse, but it was weeks. However, the day I had to go to the morgue and formally identify my child will always be yesterday. In my pocket I carried a letter from her sister, the rose quartz from Alisha's windowsill which Brianna had always coveted and often tried to take, and a pink, fluffy blanket to keep her warm.

'I just want to come home.'

I know, my baby, I know. To see her lying there, in still

repose, tucked in under a duvet, was absolutely devastating. I wanted to pick her up and take my sleeping child home. I knew that I wasn't going to be able to do that. Despite how high the duvet had been tucked up carefully around her, I could see the edges of the surgical tape. I knew what lay beneath. Twenty-eight wound dressings. I could not stay and I could not leave. I felt I was being ripped apart. My whole being cracked. How could I leave her there? The journey home from the mortuary was unbearable, and then I noticed a flash of pink in the corner of my eye. Then another. I looked up. Out of the window the cherry blossoms seemed to have burst into life. Surely they were early? It was as if the trees had magically popped. Giant cotton balls of pink on every tree, lining my way home. I may sound mad, but I felt she *was* coming home. Every bloom was Brianna. Every flash of pink was her way of telling me she was all right.

Vicky and her husband Jacob had set up a GoFundMe page which was receiving donations and messages from people as far away as Canada. Vicky would read them to me. Though it felt strange at first, it was incredible to hear so many heartfelt, generous messages, and even though most were from strangers I was comforted by them. Someone sent me a screenshot of the Warrington Wolves' hooker wearing his Number 16 shirt with Brianna's name on it, which was utterly surreal. Then the vigils started. I knew there had been a candlelit vigil on Culcheth village green organized by residents and the local choir to show their support and shock at what had happened in their usually peaceful, friendly community. I personally couldn't face going, I needed – need – to remember my child alive. But I wanted to see it. I was amazed by the sheer number of people gathering to remember Brianna, but immediately became aware of noise around her death from people who did not know her, discussing a narrative that I did not recognize. I turned off my phone. I was afraid of that darkness. I had to find the light. I was told about the other vigils taking place around the country: people had come together to stand in solidarity for a young person whose life had been violently and incomprehensibly snatched away. Dublin, Manchester, Liverpool, London's Soho Square, Lancaster and Leeds, Belfast and Birmingham – it was utterly and wonderfully overwhelming, but I didn't have the strength to go to them either.

Many of the people attending were, understandably, from the trans community, but just as many were not. The woman who had coordinated Brianna's participation in TAGS, the trans and gay support group that Brianna had for a while attended, got in touch with me. Was I happy for them to use an image of Brianna for a vigil planned in Warrington that Saturday, a week after her death? Was it only a week? It felt like a year. But I wanted to go – at least I wanted to try and go. Vicky made all the arrangements.

Brianna's friend from Scotland came all the way with her mum. We all met at Nando's, which overlooked a courtyard at the centre of the Golden Square shopping centre where the vigil was planned to take place. We could see people arriving, laying out their hand-painted signs, lighting candles. Just as we ordered, a fire alarm went off and the whole of Golden Square was evacuated. People flooded to the meeting spot, the now redundant fish market, and it filled up. I believe it was Brianna who set off the alarm. She wanted a few more people at her vigil. That or we weren't allowed Nando's without her. Either way, it made us laugh, and I had thought I would never laugh again. It felt good to laugh with her. We moved to another restaurant and they kindly kept the long window table for us so we could come and go as unnoticeably as possible. I suspect my number one angel Vicky was pulling invisible strings to make everything go as smoothly as possible. I would meet many more angels along the road, but she was there from the very start. It was beautiful to see the pictures of Brianna held up, the trans and Pride and peace flags fluttering together. People coming to say: there is good in this world, we are here to counter the darkness. There was a two-minute silence and people held up the torches on their phones and their candles and became the light. It was awe-inspiring. Brianna, you would have loved it. I looked across the sea of faces, humbled and grateful but also in so much pain.

This should not be happening.

We are not alone.

*

I had to do the unthinkable: plan my child's funeral. We kept trying to read poems and listen to music, but making any sort of decision became impossibly hard. Though I tried to keep the outside world at bay, the horror of the attack kept creeping in. Sleep was a blessed relief. I would dream of Brianna as a child, her and Alisha in the bath, her distinctive, irrepressible giggle loud in my ear. One night it was the two of them in the garden of a National Trust-style house. I stopped to sit on the ground and untangle a bunch of twigs with berries on them. One berry was white and I was trying to see what it was. I looked up and had lost sight of the kids then realized I couldn't open my eyes and I couldn't see them. I was fumbling around the place, panicked, straining to open my eyes. When I finally managed to, I was in my bedroom staring at my sunlight alarm, my heart pounding so loudly I thought I would wake Alisha next to me. I decided we needed some time away and found a little holiday cottage in Wales to rent.

The strangest things hit you. We put our bags down in the hallway of a two-bedroom holiday cottage. A double room for me and Wes, and another room with . . . Alisha and I just stared into the room. There were two beds but only one child. Every single holiday we'd ever been on, she would share a room with her noisy, annoying, beloved, funny, irreplaceable sibling. For a moment we couldn't breathe and went back outside. Alisha had been really struggling and this break was supposed to help, but it was too hard. We sank on to the bench outside the cottage and, just as we hit a new depth of realization – there was no escape from this grief – the sky painted us a picture of hope. Every cloud hovering above the wide valley below us glowed a heart-warming pink, and for a brief moment we were four again, united under a pink sky. And then that mischievous dash of humour from Bree. The bloody, stinking, noisy cows. Behind the cottage, unbeknownst to us and definitely not advertised, was a massive cow field. We smelled them before we could see them. They absolutely stank and they were making such a racket, like really bad singing donkeys. It was hilarious. Just as we were about to collapse, it was Brianna, and that cheeky snigger, that dragged us back on to our feet again. We took ourselves off and walked under that pink sky until we felt able to go back into the cottage, put on the kettle and sit down with a brew. The small moments made the biggest difference.

'I don't think I want flowers at the funeral,' I said to Alisha and Wes on a walk the next day. We had found a local independent family funeral company and secured the big Gothic church of St Elphin's because we'd decided we wanted the service to be a public one. It is not what I expected to be doing, but I wanted to honour the kind and compassionate people who had left messages and attended the vigils and, mostly, I wanted to do it for Brianna. The cremation would be private. On the funeral company's website, as well as announcing the funeral details, there was a Tribute page where people could add photos and memories. There was also a fundraising link to a charity that meant something to the person who had died, for example Alzheimer's UK, Dementia UK, Bone Marrow Transplant Units, Marie Curie, Macmillan, Air Ambulance, Hospices and Cancer Research. I liked the idea, but none of those charities applied to Brianna – but I did think donations would be better than flowers. We'd been sent so many bouquets, each one beautiful and much appreciated, but I had put so much plastic in the bin and had watched every pretty pink bloom perish and die, and I couldn't do it any more.

Once the idea of a charity was planted in my head, I decided I really wanted to do this. I didn't want to choose a big charity because I thought what little money we might raise would get lost; it wouldn't really mean anything, and I really, even then, wanted this to mean something. I couldn't bear that my child might have died for nothing. I had religiously followed my family liaison officer's advice and not listened to speculation or rumour and therefore had read nothing, seen nothing and listened to no one but her. I had not watched the news and had no idea what was being reported about Brianna's death. I must have told myself a million times, don't go on social media, do not go anywhere near it, and if you do, don't look at the comments, *do not* look at the comments.

I turned on my laptop and went on the internet. I went on social media. I looked at the comments.

It.

Was.

Horrific.

I couldn't believe what I was seeing. My daughter's murder was being discussed like it was a fictitious death in a TV show and everyone seemed happy – and dare I say it, excited – to add their thoughts to the discussion about every new piece of information like it was a new episode. I realize it was a lot to go from a news blackout to a lightning storm, but I could not understand it. I retched and bent over double, sure I was going to be sick. They had no idea of what we had been through, what we were going through and what we were trying to get through. Worse even than the animated opinions shared on a mothers' forum were the hateful and dehumanizing comments made about Brianna. Aim your vicious words at me – I am alive and can defend myself if I choose – but please, don't do that to my kid. Brianna was a proud transgender teenager with many complex needs; she was who she was and now she wasn't. What sort of person – *mother* – would find time in their precious pain-free day to put my parenting on trial while I was trying to choose a poem for my child's funeral? Up until that day, 5 March, I had received nothing but love. Now it was hate's turn, and it sliced through me like a five-inch blade. I sat back down on the bench and stared over the valley, forcing my thoughts back to the candles and prayers, the understanding and hope. The love had genuinely soothed and comforted me. I would not let the hate in. And that was my lightbulb moment.

We need to be more mindful.

Mindful of our thoughts, words and actions. And most definitely mindful of when they all come together on a keyboard. Whoever typed those comments, I am sure, I hope, didn't expect me to actually read them, but I did. It wasn't a private chat between two adults, it was a derogatory value system being beamed across the world. My child was trans – did that mean she deserved to die? I was the parent of a transgender child – did that mean I deserved to formally identify my child in a morgue? Surely those questions would have been enough to stop 99 per cent of the pile-on. I remember thinking, if adults can do this, then how the hell are we supposed to stop children from doing it? Then I thought: if children could be taught mindfulness, perhaps those future adults might be less inclined to harm themselves or others and would have some protection against the harm that is directed at them.

The thought expanded in my mind. One of Brianna's friends had bravely told me that Brianna had actively been following self-harm sites on Instagram. And pro-anorexic sites on Twitter. I hadn't been able to look at her phone – I still had holes in the walls as proof of what happened when I did – I had been more worried about who was contacting her. The friend had tried her best to dissuade Brianna from going down that rabbit hole, but Brianna had got cross and pulled away. We all knew what that felt like. I didn't want Brianna's friend to feel responsible. She couldn't stop it, I couldn't stop it, and I was just starting to understand, for the first time, what Brianna had been bombarded with. I imagined her going to her phone to ask for advice about how to cope with how she was feeling, then self-harm being suggested as a way to relieve those difficult feelings – and then the floodgates opened. She did not have the tools to resist, she went looking for help and was served up harm. I started thinking about my own lack of resilience and self-belief at that young age, and how much worse the world was now. Where was the compassion? The understanding?

How is everybody so disjointed and polarized that one group of mothers could be so lacking in compassion for another mother whose child has died that they can have a full-blown debate about whether it is my fault my child was murdered? How is it that you either belong to this group or that group and we're all so opposed that we've become tribal and vicious and dangerous? It all came tumbling into my mind that if everyone could just stop for a second and think about what we are doing to ourselves, our world and our children, then maybe we could stop another child dying. It seemed to me in that moment in Wales that it all came down to empathy. Who had it and who needed it. I knew that mindfulness had helped me find mental resilience before, and empathy towards myself and other people. If it could help me and Alisha get through this terrible time, then perhaps it could help other people, kids especially, so I ended up googling whether there was a mindfulness charity and whether mindfulness was ever taught in schools.

Mindfulness in Schools Project (MiSP) was the first thing that came up. It looked interesting and was the most established training organization in England in that field so I decided to get in touch. The first line of my email is so telling. I wanted to stay as hidden as possible. Even as I write that, I can feel Brianna pulling a face. Obviously, that didn't happen, but I stick by that email and the feelings I expressed in it even when I was at my most raw, even when I had no idea what content Brianna or her killers had been consuming for hours on their social media feeds and searches, and even when I had no idea that two fifteen-year-olds had plotted a murder on WhatsApp.

Sent: 06 March 2023 09:01

To: enquiries@mindfulnessinschools.org

Subject: Brianna Ghey

Good morning,

Please keep my email address and phone number confidential x

My name is Esther. I'm the mother of Brianna Ghey, who sadly passed away.

I'm planning Brianna's funeral and have been asked for a charity of choice for donations.

I've been passionate about mindfulness, meditation and wellbeing in my own life for many years now. **I feel that in the current world of fast-paced living, the internet and social media, children need to be taught how to have a healthy mind.**

I think that if children felt better about themselves and the world, then what happened to Brianna could have been prevented.

I found your charity through a Google search. I would like to have you as my named charity of choice. I'll see if there's a way to promote your charity using Brianna's name. **I need something good to come out of this awful situation.**

Brianna went to Birchwood High School in Warrington. I was wondering if you could offer anything to this school. I know that Brianna's death has affected the teachers and many of the students.

I look forward to hearing from you. Feel free to call me: **********

Many thanks,

Esther Ghey

I really did need something good to come out of this awful situation, and I still do. The CEO of the charity, Emily, and I had a Zoom meeting when I got back from Wales and, though I recall it all as glacial, in actual fact things moved quite fast. Nine days later we held Brianna's funeral at St

Elphin's Church. We used the money the GoFundMe page had raised to make it memorable, though I remember very little. Her Tribute page was full of beautiful messages, and donations were made to MiSP from the moment I added them to the website. I had noticed on the MiSP website that a teacher could be sponsored for £775, so I decided to aim high and try to raise enough to train three teachers. I told Emily I was going to contact some primary schools in my local area to see if they were interested. If we reached our target, we could train three, but even if we didn't, I promised Emily that I would personally make the money up if it fell short of the £2,500. With their approval, I added this text to the funeral page and also created a JustGiving page:

> *Instead of flowers for Brianna's funeral, please donate towards my chosen charity: Mindfulness in Schools Project. I'd like to sponsor a teacher in as many local schools as possible and raise awareness of the importance of taking care of mental health in our society. Brianna struggled with her mental health, and I wish that there were better resources to support her when she needed it.*

I am very proud to be able to say we've trained up a few more than three teachers.

'Will you fucking be quiet!'

A usual refrain round our house. It's the dogs, you see. They are demons. However, this didn't usually happen with a vicar sitting downstairs. Praying. The Reverend Debbie Lovat was absolutely lovely throughout the planning of the funeral. I had to admit to her that I wasn't at all religious and confessed to her that I only wanted a church service because I wanted to fit a lot of people in. She'd come over to finalize the plans, so Wes and I tried to do that thing we'd seen on TV, laying out cups and saucers, a plate of biscuits in the middle of the table, pouring tea from the pot. I couldn't look Wes in the eye. The reverend asked us what hymns we wanted, and we must have looked at her blankly because she suggested 'Amazing Grace'. I thought: Oh well, I know 'Amazing Grace', so let's choose that one. Afterwards, she suggested we say a prayer, so we all sat there quietly, and that's when Alisha started screaming at the dogs. Brianna would have loved that.

There were some terrible moments that pierced through the blanket of sadness. Taking a bag of clothes to the funeral parlour for them to dress Brianna in was beyond horrendous. Alisha and I chose her pink – no longer fluffy but beloved – pyjama bottoms and a pink Barbie T-shirt. We wanted her to be comfortable. The lady who helped us was another angel, making the hardest moments somehow bearable. She referred to the casket as a bed, and I knew Brianna would be gently and lovingly dressed for sleep, covered in the blanket, in her favourite, most comfortable clothes. This was our Brianna. The one who lounged about with the dogs, cracking jokes and generally taking the piss out of one of us.

She really was around. I know that sounds crazy, but she was. Even at the funeral, which was terrible and mad at the same time, there were touches of her that I could almost hear her orchestrating from wherever she was. Our family and her few chosen friends got into four limousines and we followed the white horse-drawn carriage on to the road. Two grey horses with pink feather plumes pulled the coffin to the church. There was one ridiculously slow horse – we were definitely holding up the traffic that busy Saturday afternoon.

'I really hope that nobody's in a rush because no one's getting anywhere with this bloody horse.'

Somehow, it made us laugh, because who loved an entrance more than Brianna? I kept thinking of the footage from the last family wedding we went to. There she was in her pink dress and long nails, hair extensions and make-up, and she turned the phone on to herself.

'Here I am, the star of the show!'

With people lining the streets, queuing to get in and out of the church, the touches of pink everywhere, I thought, yes, my love, you bloody well are.

When I walked in I had my head down. I didn't want to see anybody in that sea of people, I just needed to get to my place. The bells tolled. Then they were matched with the opening church bells of Lana Del Ray's 'Video Games'. Harp strings filled the space, then those exalting chords.

It is coming up to two years without her and I still cannot listen to music. It simply undoes me.

Sitting in that church, I could not fathom that I had to leave my child soon, but once again, when I needed reassurance the most, it came from her. It was the hymn that did it. 'Amazing Grace'. It is so high that there was no way I could sing it. The person standing next to me – turned out it was the Mayor of Warrington – was doing a really good job, but all I could think of was that Bree would be wincing at the terrible noise we were making.

'Oh my God, you're all so embarrassing.'

I know, right.

It's okay: she was still with me.

This should not be happening.

Her friends spoke movingly, and I was bowled over by their bravery. I noticed the pink. I couldn't look at the coffin, though now I am acutely aware that we chose the one with pink clouds on it. Of course. As ever, Brianna making her presence felt. She would not be forgotten. I only know what was said now because I have read the words so often and I can bypass the service and stand in the shoes of the people who knew her and loved her for who she was.

You are not alone.

Brianna's headteacher, Emma Mills, stood at the lectern.

She said, 'At school, we will all miss Brianna's bravery and courage. We will miss her determination and grit. We will miss her wit and her humour. We will even miss her insults and her putting us all in our place, as she so loved to do.

'We are so glad that Brianna came to join us at Birchwood – we are so glad that she was part of our school community, as we learned so much from her. We learned so much about strength and determination to be one's true self – and that is something that we will all carry with us. She was a true one-off, unique and truly unforgettable. What a privilege it was to know her.'

And suddenly it was time for a last poem.

May the roads rise to meet you
May the wind be always at your back
May the sunshine warm upon your face
The rain fall soft, upon you
And until we meet again
Be assured
You are always in our thoughts
Say not in grief they are no more
But live in thankfulness that they were.

We will live in thankfulness that you were here, I vowed, as 'Somewhere over the Rainbow' started playing and I knew the terrible time had come for her to be taken from the church and transferred to the hearse for our final drive together. Could we just press pause? I wasn't ready to say goodbye. How do you say goodbye? This was agony. I thought it could not get worse than this moment. But the torture would continue.

Later, at the wake, we filled the room with light and pink balloons, determined to make it a celebration.

'It's more like a wedding than a funeral,' said her sister, and she was right. Somehow we would both find the strength to celebrate Brianna's life rather than being crippled by the fact that she is not here. It is a tightrope I have walked every day since and the reason why, when the council asked me if I would agree to them putting a memorial bench in the place where she died, I said no. It is her life I wish to recall. Not her death. Life and love. Not death and hate.

Brianna and I are running through hallways. I am just behind her. Then she reaches a door, her hair swings around her face, she glances back at me through those thick lenses she'd had since she was six, flashes her model smile and disappears through the door. It closes shut behind her. I reach it; I push. I push and push, I start banging on the door, I am screaming her name.

'Mum!'

It was Alisha, I was sat bolt upright in bed, screaming, my heart pounding. No, no, I had to go back, I couldn't leave her, I had to . . .

'Mum!'

I looked at Alisha. A new feeling settled over me and I knew what it meant.

'She's gone,' I said.

I think Brianna stuck around until she was happy we could look after ourselves and each other. By then we were on a mission to leave the world a safer place, and we were going to do it in the name of the one and only, a girl of our time, Brianna Ghey.

14

Something Good Must
Come of This

Fifteen days after the funeral, I was invited by Emma Mills to come to the school to plant a tree in Brianna's memory. It was a cherry tree, of course. I appreciated the idea, but when I woke up that morning I really didn't want to go. I was feeling incredibly tired, like someone had ironed me flat. But a local cake company had donated all these beautiful pink cakes to sell for MiSP and I didn't want to let anyone down. Alisha didn't come with me. She was finding it all very hard, especially other people's reactions. I thought I could soldier on, but I found that day extremely challenging. I was trying to get back to 'normal', but it wasn't working.

When I finally went back to work, it was horrendous. The last time I'd been in the office I'd been getting about five phone calls a day from school, but now – nothing. The phone no longer rang and the texts no longer came. I couldn't handle it. It was too obvious that Brianna wasn't in my life any more. I couldn't be the worker I had been, so I handed in my notice.

Being at home was just as bad. The house was too quiet. The thing is, my homebird had always been there, chattering away into her phone or filming something. I could hear her through the thin wall that separates our rooms. How many times had I asked her to turn down the volume while I tried to meditate at the end of the day? The pain that radiates through my body when I remember those times is impossible to describe. It is visceral. Sometimes I would place my ear to the wall and wait, praying, hoping for the impossible. That I would hear her again.

'She wouldn't want to be in the dirt,' said a friend. She wouldn't want to be in the dark either. Or alone. The donations we'd been sent meant I could redecorate Brianna's room and make it a pink palace of peace. It is where she felt most comfortable, so we decided we would make it her final resting place. It is very beautiful and there is a special place for the box of ashes with the same pink clouds her casket had, and the rose quartz is in there too. In her newly painted room there is a pink, fluffy rug that I never allowed her to have when she was alive because she was always spilling things and it would have been ruined in a matter of days. Heartbreakingly, her room is always pristine now. In those early days I spent a long time sitting in there, looking at the wall of photos of happy times from her life, scrolling through photos and videos, just to hear her voice.

One of my favourites, which I played over and over,

was a video she made me after one of our most vicious arguments. Brianna had a pretty big following by that time, enough to mean that companies and brands were approaching her to promote their products. One was a 'professional' home hair-removal machine. Of course, to review it, she had to be sent it, and to be sent it she had to give out our home address. I was so nervous about who she was communicating with online that I really didn't want her giving our address out to anyone, ever. What if it was a dodgy product or, worse, being sent by someone who wanted to harm my trans child? I was terrified about acid attacks. My mum offered for the thing to be sent to her house instead. So Brianna went over there to pick it up and filmed herself using it, to prove it was safe. I was furious at the time, but it is a treasure now.

'Hi, Mum.'

You can hear my mum pottering about in the background. 'What's that, love?' she asked Brianna from the kitchen.

'I'm speaking to Mum.'

That's the bit I listen to. Hi, Mum. Hi, Mum. I have no one to say 'I told you so' to, but when I looked at the machine closely I realized that the brand name, which should have been KENZi, actually had a second i at the end. It was counterfeit, badly made, it got very hot and burnt her skin. I tried to report it, but got nowhere; no customer support, of course. She wasn't a customer. She was a target. I know I am a natural-born worrier – Brianna called me a stress-head a lot of the time, and I am – that's why I have worked so hard not to fall into the pattern of negative thinking. It has never served me. But when I recall the many horrible scenarios I feared for Brianna, being stabbed by a friend was not one of them.

After her death, I could have sent myself crazy, so I forced myself not to ruminate on the limited information I had. Every ounce of mental resilience my mindfulness practice had given me helped me stay afloat on an ocean of grief. I focused on the cherry blossoms that seemed to be multiplying in size and quantity and were blooming in a Technicolor pink. Outside the window it looked like Barbie World. If that was a sign, I would cling to it and I would find the strength to plant that tree. But I was hanging on by my fingernails.

It was Emily, the CEO of MiSP, who first suggested some extra mindfulness training for me. They were incredibly grateful I had chosen them as a charity and we had formed a mutually supportive bond very quickly. While I had a reasonable amount to do, there were still too many hours in the day where I could be pulled into a dark and dangerous place. I think they realized that while I would say I was doing okay, it was evident I was struggling. The course they offer is eight weeks of training. In a group. They worried I wasn't ready for that, and again, they were right, so in the meantime they suggested I do a few one-to-one sessions just to help me through the difficult days.

Introducing the angel that is Faiy. She helped me on a fundamental level, and she helps me now. At our first meeting we both sobbed. She's not trained in trauma or how to deal with somebody who has experienced a horrific loss, so for her to offer and show such exceptional kindness was life-changing. I would like to take this opportunity to acknowledge that kindness. I am not sure I would have got through the investigation, the pre-trial hearing or the trial without her. She was a life raft in human form.

It had been Wes's idea to do the Great North Swim. He said it would be a good way to take care of my mental health and also to keep us busy. This is a man who is happiest caring for his family and being out in nature, so I should have seen it coming. Wes is a keen open-water swimmer and we'd started doing it during lockdown, though most of the time I would stubbornly say no to joining him, but on this occasion I thought he might be on to something. I liked the idea of having a goal, a reason to get in the water, and I understood the link between swimming in nature and improving mental health. The more I thought about it, the more I felt it ticked a lot of boxes for me personally, and it gave us another opportunity to raise some money for MiSP. I contacted the Great North Swim about getting caps made with MiSP on them. Undeterred when I didn't hear back from them, I decided to get in touch with Tom Bedworth from the *Warrington Guardian* to see if I could drum up some support.

Tom, I had been told, had covered our case from the beginning, and though I hadn't read any of it myself, people told me he had been honestly and respectfully writing about the investigation while always keeping Brianna front and centre in a caring and sensitive way, never forgetting a child had lost their life. I emailed him to find out whether he would consider promoting our fundraising for MiSP in the *Warrington Guardian*. Tom immediately offered his support and we set up an interview at the Engine Rooms, a café in the centre of the landscaped business park near where we live. It is that park where the photo of Brianna eating a chocolate bar was taken, it has a stunning duck pond that always makes me think of her and a Zen garden that I visit to collect my thoughts and have a moment out of what are now busy days. Thanks to the business park, I run my Community Interest Company called Peace & Mind UK from an office they gave me to use, but back then, the café was the only place I could face going. I didn't want anyone coming to our house, but I couldn't handle big spaces or crowds. Little did people know then that within a few short months they wouldn't be able to get rid of me! I sat down with Tom and he started asking me questions, then scribbling indecipherable marks in his notebook. I was all over the place. I had only done one other interview and it had been very hardcore, and obviously, before that, I'd never done anything like this. I was a bit freaked out and a tad paranoid about what those scribbles meant. Needless to say, I shouldn't have worried. Tom is a joy of a human being and someone I appreciate being able to talk to, even if he has now abandoned me for the BBC! He definitely falls into the angel category and deserves to succeed. He was a brilliant advocate for me, my family and our town.

I was cautious about putting myself out there, for one very good reason. On Sunday, 7 May I got an automatically generated email from the MuchLoved tribute website informing me that someone had started their own fundraiser for MiSP. Excited that word was spreading, I clicked on the page. Instead of fluttering memorial candles and kind words, there were pages and pages of images of decapitated bodies, erections and graphic, horrific images of violent acts. I slammed the laptop lid down, shocked, panicking and shaking. I didn't know what to do. This was a precious place where people had gone to write lovely messages and upload their photos which I'd never seen before, so it wasn't as simple as shutting it down. I wanted to keep those pictures and memories; they brought me comfort. I know it was a Sunday because I thought I had no hope of getting anyone to help, but thankfully someone responded to my panicked message. They told me how to delete the messages I didn't like. I told her to go and look at the page herself – it wasn't just a few pictures I didn't like. It was a flood of horror, and I pleaded with them not to make me do that. There was no way I could face that.

I could tell the person at MuchLoved was left reeling from the sheer quantity of images. She kindly took everything down.

By Monday morning the company had changed all the settings. It was my first lesson on what can be done to protect vulnerable people (me) from seeing harmful content (sickeningly violent and unsolicited sexual images). First they made it private and password protected. They also made sure the people who had posted nice things could still be part of the tribute page through an automatically created invitation, and lastly, and most interestingly to me, they added a filter that meant I was automatically emailed a copy of anything anyone wanted to add and the person adding to the page would be informed that I would then need to 'accept' the contribution. By omission, it was telling any would-be spammers or trolls that the site was being effectively monitored. We had no more porn uploaded after that. What a difference consequences make, I thought, and what a difference content moderation makes. This was a relatively small website attached to a local funeral home. Imagine what a trillion-dollar company could do if it put its weighty technical mind to it. Why don't they, I wondered?

The page was rescued, but it left a sour taste in my mouth and a repetitive thought in my mind. Who does that? And why? I would have liked to call them out, let them know how grievously it had hurt me, but I couldn't. They hadn't left a number or email, or even their name. It was from about this time that I started to ask myself why anyone should ever be allowed to post anything anonymously. An email address should be as valuable, as identifiable, as your passport. Or linked to a tax code. It would be a public portal to who you are as a person, what you stand for. You are welcome to your hates and disagreements, but it has to be you voicing them to the world. It would mean humans and bots could be immediately differentiated, it would mean SpaceMonkey69 could not flood the Tribute page dedicated to the memory of a murdered sixteen-year-old with images so vile it makes me sick to think of it, even now.

In the immediate aftermath, I couldn't get the images out of my head. The thought of going public with a campaign made me worry for myself and my family and made me feel extremely protective of Brianna. I wanted to curl into a ball and hide and, for about a day, I did. I didn't have the strength to go out and face the world, I would have to tell Tom that I couldn't do it. But slowly something happened and this 'fuck that' feeling started to build in me. These were the very people I was doing this for, people who needed more empathy and compassion in their lives, and I would find the strength to get off the sofa from all the extraordinary support I had received from the people of Warrington and further afield. Every thoughtful message reminded me that love and kindness still existed, and if we worked together we could build a society in which such a murder could not happen. I had a massive hole in my heart: either I could let the love pour into it and heal it, or I could let the hate make the hole so big it swallowed me whole.

The *Warrington Guardian* article came out on 25 May with some lovely pictures of Brianna and smiley ones of Wes and me looking a bit daft in our wetsuits, and suddenly, seeing it all in print, it became very real. We were no longer talking about changing things, change had begun. It was a good feeling, and I was grateful for it. We had been so generously supported by people near and far, I did feel that this was one way we could not only do something positive in Brianna's name but also repay that generosity by doing something proactive to improve mental health in our society. We had worked hard to get the wording right for the fundraiser, and I still stick by that message.

Taking care of our mental health is more important than ever. The fast pace in which we live, along with an over-reliance on social media and recovering from the Covid lockdowns has had a massive impact on our health and wellbeing.

By bringing mindfulness into schools we can help children and teachers to build mental resilience and help to strengthen empathy towards themselves and others. Let's have a go at building a happier future.

I was happy to admit that Brianna had struggled. She was neither the bullied victim, as some were claiming, nor the singularly happy, confident girl strutting her stuff. She was, as we all are, so much more than that. The article printed the link for my JustGiving page, and the donations started coming in. Each one with a message of hope and encouragement. I felt buoyed by the whole thing, though realized I hadn't yet done the swim.

On 10 June Alisha stayed at home to look after the dogs and Wes and I set off to get to Lake Windermere. It did not start well. Wes was confident about how long the drive would take, but I was thinking, we need to be setting off much earlier than that, or we'll be cutting it too fine. We cut it too fine. It was a really hot day, there were cars parked everywhere, so we drove to the hotel, then carried all our stuff back to the registration tent, which felt like miles. I was sweating like a pig when we finally got there. Then we had to get into our wetsuits, by which time I was effing and blinding and in a foul, foul mood because I couldn't get the bloody tracker around my fat ankle. We had to run to the start line having missed the warm-up and the health and safety briefing, and so when we got to the lake we were right at the back, which was fine, but there were so many people there to support, and I was standing there in my wetsuit and swimming cap, face like thunder, thinking, please God can nobody take a picture.

The reason why I am writing this is not to describe the

barney that was taking place while I was dressed as a seal, but because, and I promise this is true, as soon as we got into the water, I felt better. The calm, still water carried me. Oh, it's all right. I'm all right. The angst floated away and I started focusing on my breathing and my swimming. I knew I was back to myself when all my energy went into one thing. Beating Wes. In case you're interested, I did. Beat him, that is. By about ten minutes. I know we were lucky, because the following year, when we did two miles, the water was so choppy people were getting dragged out of the water. After the swim we went back to our beautiful hotel Low Wood Bay to be told we'd got an upgrade. Another stroke of luck. We went to the spa, ate delicious food and went to bed happy, already excited about break-fast the next day. I do love a hotel breakfast.

It did not disappoint – that breakfast buffet had every-thing – but I was finding it hard. It was the music playing in the dining room, as since Brianna had died, as I said, I found music almost unbearable. I've only just recently started being able to listen to music of any kind, but sad music still makes me cry.

'You want to go?' asked Wes. No, I told him, there was smoked salmon; I wasn't going to pass up a chance to eat that! I was just about dealing with it when a woman came and sat on the table next to us. She had two little red-headed children, a girl and a boy. I completely broke down. I covered my face in the big white napkin, thinking, I'll be all right in a minute. I didn't want to ruin breakfast, but the explosion of emotions was enormous. I kept looking over, thinking, I wish that was me again. What would I give? What wouldn't I give? A memory flooded back.

'Don't put the pastries in the moving toast rack.'

Cut to . . . alarm bells. Real ones. All the guests being evacuated. I look at my giggling, grinning, grimacing child. Why is a waiter running towards the buffet with a fire extinguisher? Oops. Honestly, Brianna, you were a rule breaker from the start. The funny, cute memories are bitter, bittersweet because they make me miss her more. Just thinking about seeing those kids with their mum makes me feel emotionally raw. Even now, it's the unexpected moments that I find the hardest.

During that first meeting with Tom Bedford, he asked me if I had ever thought about running an official campaign that we could launch in our area. I wasn't sure what he was suggesting so we talked more about creating something the *Warrington Guardian* could actively support that would augment what I was doing for MiSP. Make it official. If I was interested in that, he would go back and speak to his boss.

'I am interested,' I told him, while having absolutely no idea what I was talking about.

'Great. We're going to need a name,' said Tom, without taking a breath. Now I was really panicking, I'd never campaigned before – I didn't even know what campaigning entails. I kept thinking, I'm not capable of something like this.

'That's not true, Mum . . .' I looked out of the window of the Engine Rooms, across the manicured, undulating lawn, across to the duck pond. Sometimes she was so close, if I could turn fast enough, I'd catch her. She was right: I'd battled and overcome a drug addiction. With the help of mindfulness I had stopped feeling hopeless and ruminating on those terrible teenage years and had instead learned to enjoy the present and look positively to the future. I had taken myself back to school, studied nutrition, had taken a job before I was even qualified and had become a product developer. If I could pull myself out of a dark place and build a better future for my children then, I could do it again. I rolled my eyes: she was still pushing, still nagging, still a pain in the arse. I could imagine her faint cackle. 'A campaign in my name, love it.'

Tom and I did a quick brainstorm and we both felt this was an opportunity both locally for our schools but also to make a lasting difference by maybe weaving mindfulness into the school day. Emma and I had been talking about it since I'd landed on MiSP, and she felt strongly that it would really help reduce the overwhelming number of children who were presenting with mental health problems. Tom came back with a big thumbs-up from his bosses, so we were good to go. All we needed was a name and a mission statement. Peace of Mind was taken, so Peace & Mind was born. I designed the logo, a cherry tree in blossom with a pink bow tied round it. In homage to Brianna. Overnight I became a campaigner in my child's name, and from then things moved fast, then faster and still faster. I re-read the emails, and it's staggering how much we achieved in such a short time.

Our local rugby team, the Warrington Wolves, did not hesitate to get involved. A lot of things lined up. It wasn't just that Danny Walker, the hooker who had worn the Brianna Number 16 shirt, was an anti-knife crime advocate, but the wellbeing manager of the Wolves, the exceptional James Howes, was passionate about mindfulness and about Warrington. He loved the idea of investing in mindfulness training in every primary school across the town. The idea was simple, really. Increase compassion, decrease violence. Now we had to spread the word. Warrington Wolves already employed the dynamic, effervescent Claire Gamble as their community engagement officer. There was nothing these two energetic, soulful humans couldn't do. Being in their presence was humbling, exciting and daunting all at the same time, and I was bowled over by their spirit and enthusiasm from the first moment we met. It was all 'we can do this and that, and maybe this and why not that?' Warrington is a big rugby league town, the game was already being taught in every primary school, so they had the reach, the know-how, and it was clear to me they had the desire to help. Having them in our corner was massive and it one hundred per cent freaked me out.

'So,' they said, 'when do we launch?' We were sitting in their offices in July. Wait, what? Hang on . . . I had butterflies in my stomach. Not the good kind, the kind that make you want to run out of the room and be violently sick in the nearest toilet. I nearly did. I nearly put the brakes on right then and there. I wasn't ready. I couldn't do this. I was still being updated on the investigation, the toll was terrible, the trolling scared me. And then Brianna did it again.

'Well, we have a big game on 15 September against St Helen's – why not launch the Peace & Mind campaign then? Everyone can wear your new pink blossom T-shirts, even the mascot. It's being televised – it will be huge!'

Of all the dates. How could I refuse now? The 15th of September is my birthday, and this was a gift I could not turn down.

On the day, I got to the stadium before 6 a.m. so we could do our first live interview 'down the line', a terrifying experience which entailed staring down the large, dark eye of a camera on the edge of a deserted pitch while talking to a miniature Kate Garraway and Ben Shephard on a screen. I had been lucky enough to meet Russell Treasure, the Warrington Wolves mindfulness coach. He and I had definitely drunk the same Kool-Aid and we believed that mindfulness had saved our lives. He had offered to come in early and do a guided meditation with me and he managed to get me to concentrate on the sound, movement and the temperature of my breath, but honestly, I was a basket case. Russell uses exercises to drag and then anchor the worrying mind into the present, where usually there is nothing to worry about, but in this case my present meant stepping in front of a camera and talking live on national TV. He's good, don't get me wrong, but I was jangling. It felt like I was driving down a pot-holed road with no suspension. Emma and I nipped into a box to put on some slap, and I was now so nervous I took two paracetamols. The thing is, Emma was used to standing up and speaking to people, but I do not have that sort of confidence, I'd never done any public speaking and now I was about to speak live into a TV camera.

'I don't think I can do this. I don't know what to say.'

'You'll be fine,' said Emma reassuringly. 'Just get the link to the website in.'

The next thing I knew we were wired up and both had Kate Garraway and Ben Shephard talking in our ears. It was mad. I could not look at Emma – I was either going to cry or get uncontrollable nervous giggles. To make things even more weird, Tom, Claire, James and Russell were sitting in front of us in the huge, empty stadium watching us in person and also live on their phones.

I watched the interview back the other day. I look like a rabbit in headlights, and it feels like five years ago. I mumble something about aiming to get mindfulness into all schools in the UK, then realize I've gone too big too early and pull back.

'Starting with Warrington. Then get the curricul—' I can't quite get the word out. So I try again. 'The curriculum changed.' I am terrified. Now Emma looks like she's about to get the giggles and I am clearly not breathing . . . my eyes are getting wider and wider. Ben asks me to explain what mindfulness is . . .

Oh God, when will this end . . .

'It helps you live in the future' – no, that's wrong – 'It stops you worrying about the future or getting stuck in the past; it's a tool in your armoury.'

I think Kate decided it was time to help me out.

'Has it helped you to try and do something good?'

'It's really helped, keeping busy with something that is so positive . . .' My voice cracked – it's the 'positive' that gets me. Emma subtly put her hand around my back, trying to hold me up.

'Sorry.'

Once again, the pros came to my rescue and asked Emma about Brianna. I heard snippets of it while trying to get myself together. Larger than life. Vivacious. Strong-willed and funny, we miss her one-liners. Emma talks about how Brianna had been an inspiration to other students, kids who, thanks to her, found it easier to voice their own issues around gender questioning and sexuality.

'The corridors are quieter without her.' Emma always had

a way to describe Brianna faithfully without too much sugar-coating. In the hours after Brianna was named in the press, the school board had offered to write a press release for Emma, who was inundated with calls from parents, trying to quash the rumour mill and taking care of some understandably distressed children in her school. When she read about the much-loved student who was looking forward to her exams, she thought I would read that and think Emma was taking the piss. She re-wrote it, describing Brianna honestly while adding that she was quick-witted and funny, but she wasn't always the perfect student. I'll say. When Emma was asked why mindfulness would help, she delivered a pitch-perfect answer.

'Post-pandemic, there has been a myriad of issues within schools. Attendance is down and safeguarding issues have layers of complexities that we haven't seen before. The online world that the pupils relied on during the pandemic is now causing unprecedented problems. Every mistake they make is on a huge platform. If you make a mistake, there is trolling and hate. You have to be perfect and, if you're not perfect, there is trolling and hate.'

I talked a bit about how I was doing and that I believed in people, I believed we could be good to each other, and then the interview was over and Kate Garraway was saying goodbye, but I hadn't mentioned our website, so I did what you never should do on live television and interrupted the host – sorry, Kate – but at least I managed to get our details on air!

Everyone wore our new pink Peace & Mind T-shirts, even Wolfie – the team mascot – and Danny Walker wore one while he was doing his warm-up on the pitch. We had a stall with leaflets and were taking donations. Before the match I went through to the members' lounge and was interviewed by a local comedian. There was a big QR code on the screen as well, for donations to the GoFundMe page, and the whole thing was televised by Sky. I could not have asked for better support – it felt like we had the weight of the whole club behind us and it made me proud to be part of something positive. I looked over at Tom and smiled. We gave each other a thumbs-up. He helped rebuild my faith in humanity.

15

Joint Enterprise

A couple of weeks before the trial started, Wes and I went to the police station in Warrington and sat down with DCI Nige Parr and DC Sarah Newton, our brilliant liaison officer, to go through the thick sequence of events file. We were told that the two children had categorically denied having anything to do with Brianna's death in their first interviews. Yes, they had gone to the park with her, but she'd upped and left after getting a text from some seventeen-year-old boy from Manchester. The girl had told the police she'd been quite pissed off. It was her mother who had called the police station the next day, Sunday 12 February, to tell the police that her daughter had gone to the park with Brianna and hoped the information might be helpful. The information wasn't helpful. It was an absolute pack of lies. But her mother had no idea.

Their respective denials started to look very hollow as soon as the text messages they had carefully deleted and must have thought were irrecoverable were in fact recovered. It was incredibly hard reading those texts for the first time.

It was the hideously jocular, easy, excitable manner in which they discussed the murder. There were so many messages, going back as far as August 2022, swapping increasingly sickening plans to kill someone, anyone, anyhow. They had a kill list and on it were five names. Boy R because he nearly got her expelled and was gay. Boy E because he was a 'nonce'. Boy C because he'd spammed her boyfriend with death threats. Boy S made it on to the list because he showed her boyfriend a video that was offensive. And lastly Boy M because he was ruining the other defendant's chances with the girl he liked but was too shy to talk to.

At no point in the reams of texts the police recovered did either of them ever try to put on the brakes, check with the other that these plans were pretend, or demonstrate anything other than escalating excitement. If it was all just fantasy, a shared joke, there was no let up and no laughter. Almost more jarring than the depravity and thirst to kill was the mundane, everyday tone of the exchanges between them; it sent a physical bolt of shock through me. These were schoolkids who had chosen to kill another schoolkid. They were not monsters, monsters don't exist. In fact, they were alarmingly ordinary.

Girl: *Lets kill her tomorrow at 6pm*
Boy: *I can't because it's a school night*

By offering to skim over certain bits and avoiding others, Cheshire Police tried to protect us from the worst, but it was an impossible task. I didn't want to know what would be disclosed in court, but equally I had to know what Brianna had been through. However hard and brutal that was, as her mother I needed to feel she was no longer alone in her suffering. I needed to feel that I had been right there with her, and however painful it was to me, the pain was nothing compared to the terror and blinding agony she must have felt.

Girl: *I want to see the pure horror on her face and hear her scream in pain.*

The police suggested breaks often, but Wes and I only took one, when we both stood in the visitors' toilets and wept in each other's arms. I remember that we actively pulled ourselves together, drawing on one another's strength, so we could get it done and get out of there. Wes drove me home, in the dark in total silence, as I stared out of the window thinking one thing: how can I sit in a room with the people who killed my child? Having been through the sequence of events file, I knew for certain that they had.

Girl: *Meet me at the wooden posts in linear at 12 well go over plan again and ill show you where im killing her and then we both walk to the library to meet her . . . and grab onto Brianna slit her throat when she starts to fall stab her in the back then pass me knife I want to stab her at least once even if shes dead jus coz its fun lol*

We were in the public gallery above Court Room 2, slightly separated by a section of corrugated plastic which meant I could only see the tops of the defendants' heads. I think it also helped me put up an emotional barrier between myself and what was happening below. Courts were full of terrible cases, it wasn't just my family; maybe it wasn't my family at all, just another tragic case that was happening to someone else. I also had a forcefield around me. Vicky. Wes. His mum. Alisha's stepmother Laura. Emma Mills. We were all together, stuck like glue.

The jurors were picked and sworn in, then the CPS started with the outline of their case. I knew there was no doubt that the defendants were the ones seen by witnesses in the park. One woman had recognized the girl from school and had called the police to tell them her name. The dog-walkers who called 999 just after they had run away had identified them. Lastly, there was no doubt about who was in the CCTV footage of the three of them walking into the park, and the dashcam footage of only two of them running out. Yet they both maintained their innocence. If both were to be believed, neither had stabbed Brianna, each saying the other one killed her. Cowards, I thought. I had seen the file; I knew what was coming: the endless terrible texts between them, the forensic evidence and the stupid fact that they left the snacks and drinks they had been recorded buying at Sainsbury's strewn around the path.

Girl: *Lets have two words, one for getting the knife ready and another to stab.*

Girl: *For get knife ready I will look at you and cough and to stab I'll say gay. I want to see the pure horror on her face and hear her scream in pain.*

I had been shown the first responders' gut-wrenching witness statements, the air ambulance paramedic's description of the catastrophic wounds, the forensic pathology report, the autopsy; I had seen the knife and the digital reconstruction of the injuries, how many, how deep. There were wounds that were likely to be single-handed, deep and required real strength. There were others, shallower, with no bias to left or right-handed gestures, signifying a double-handed strike. The barrister was right: this was a sustained and violent assault. My liaison officer would warn me what was about to be discussed in minute detail and gave me the option to leave court so I didn't have to go through it all again. Going through the sequence of events file was hard enough but now the two people who had planned that sustained and violent attack and seen it through were sitting just under my feet.

They were trying to refute what they had done by blaming each other, and that was why we were all sitting in court, being put through this agonizing torture of a public recounting of the last terrible minutes of my child's life. They could have saved themselves, their families and mine that unerasable ordeal but at least now the speculation was over and the facts had been laid bare. Still they childishly, selfishly and cowardly thought they could bluff their way through it and there would be no accountability for any of it, at all. I had felt some sympathy for them before the trial started because they had ruined their own lives as well as ours by ending Brianna's, but over the days in court that sympathy slipped out of me. Their casual disregard for the pain and suffering they had caused us all, including their families, is not something I needed to forgive. I just needed not to hate them for it. When the boy was asked what his plea was, he wrote two words on a piece of paper and held it up. NOT GUILTY. And so the lying began.

There was a text exchange between them on 12 February, shortly before they were arrested.

> Girl: *Do you have anxiety about getting caught.*
> Boy: *Probably*
> Girl: *Youre not going to get caught, dont worry, police are shite here, I haven't been caught and I m a lot less intelligent than you.*

A lot less, I would agree. Did she really think sending Brianna a text shortly after they had killed her would be enough to cover her tracks?

Girl, is everything okay? Some teenag girl got killed in linear park its on news everywhere

Did their families believe their claims of innocence? I can understand why each family would prefer it was the other child who was capable of such a horrific attack. They were sitting in the courtroom; they would soon see and hear all that I had already seen and heard, but with their beloved and treasured children sitting right there in front of them. A different sort of agony, but agony nonetheless. At one point I walked past the girl's parents on my way to the toilet, and they looked so scared and broken. I had a strong urge to go up to them, but they would always look away, and I didn't think it was my place. During those terrible weeks I thought about the parents a lot, and how awful it must be to sit through all the evidence against their children. At what point did they realize their child had lied to them too?

The respective defences, I thought, were weak in the face of overwhelming evidence. The girl basically said all the texts, the notes and plans had been fantasy, nothing more. The boy said he was merely going along with the game and never thought she would go through with it. He didn't actually say anything; instead, he typed, because by this point he'd become a selective mute. It's not that he couldn't talk; he chose not to talk. In his first interview in police custody he'd been quite chatty. He had told his arresting officers he could explain everything and he started to spin quite a tale, insisting he did not bring a knife to the park, that he'd only been joking when he dehumanized

Brianna in his texts, claiming that he was just going along with the girl because he didn't want to lose her as a friend, but also that he never told her to stop because he was scared of her because of what he'd seen. They asked him what he had seen. He changed tack. Not seen. Heard. But after the interviewing officer described the results of the forensic tests and that day's post-mortem, his legal representative suggested a break. He was rather less chatty after that and it was 'no comment' for the rest of the interview.

At the pivotal and meticulously planned moment, the girl said she went to 'stretch her legs' and he typed that he had gone to *relieve himself behind a tree*. So after months of planning, buying a weapon, practising stabbing furniture with a knife, faking a drug-deal and pretending the fictional dealer was coming to the park, inventing a story about a boy from Manchester, inventing codewords, going over the plan, and locating the perfect remote spot to kill and then hide a body, while possibly keeping a memento, she'd gone for a walk and he'd gone for a piss. And by the way, it had never been a real plan, it was a game of fantasy. Like Warhammer. She said that while she was stretching her legs she heard a noise, like someone screaming, then she turned around and saw the boy stab Brianna. He typed that while he was peeing he'd heard a noise like something hitting the ground and had turned around and seen the girl stab Brianna. I retreated into myself. They were not talking about my baby. All this, all of it, had happened to some other unfortunate family.

Because the defendants were still so young and had differing needs, the days were shorter and there were regular breaks. Our liaison officer would escort us through the courthouse so we didn't cross paths with anyone we didn't want to. It was very choreographed and I was immensely grateful for that. While in that break room, we didn't talk about what we'd just heard or seen. We talked about nice things. We talked about silly things and had a laugh. I needed to know it was possible to feel something other than misery, that even though terrible things happen, you can still find the joy. Those breaks really helped. Then Sarah would come down and tell us it was time to go back up again. Sometimes she'd join us for a natter, and she was masterful in knowing when and how to lighten the tone and it was often she who got the most laughs out of us. I knew I was lucky to have my friends to support me. I felt safe and loved and protected by them all, and I know it helped me get through each day. Not that I needed to be reminded, but to me it proved how important community and real-life human contact is. It's not that it made everything bearable or easier, but it gave me the strength to bear it.

The days when the defendants were feeling too anxious to attend court they were allowed to stay in their residential units. For me, these sessions were especially difficult because I could see their expressions when they were on video link. The crocodile tears from the girl about seeing her friend hurt were hard to take. So much of what she said was untrue, and I didn't buy his selective mutism and the fidget toys and puzzles he was allowed; it just annoyed me. The police had told me that in the hours before his arrest the boy had been searching out symptoms of ASD and anxiety, plus information about witnessing and investigating a crime. His explanation for this was that he was trying to work out what he felt and how he could help the police, except he didn't help the police. Instead, this 'good, moral boy' lied. The process of typing his answers and it being read out by another person felt performative, as did his whole defence, to be honest. The gallery was packed with journalists. There were so many watching, the proceedings were video-linked to another room packed with more journalists. Law students came and watched. There were times when it felt like a full house at a hot, bustling theatre and we were all waiting for the curtain to rise on the show. The boy's defence barrister certainly appeared to be enjoying his time in the limelight. I wanted to leap out of my chair and scream, this is not a play, this is not a TV drama, this is the end of my child's life you are peacocking and parrying over! The drama isn't between the two defendants. The drama is that my child is dead. I gripped the chair and forced myself to listen even when I thought it was utter bullshit. I would not comment or complain because this had to be a fair trial with no possible chance of appeal. I could not go through this again.

I can't remember when I was first told about joint

enterprise or when I realized how crucial that would be to the case. A lot of things didn't register with me; all I was thinking was please, please, let's get these terrible people in prison. It was a long slog. In fact, at one point we were told that if it went on much longer we might have to wait until after Christmas for the verdict, and the thought of that was extremely stressful. Christmas was going to be hard enough. The prosecution was followed by hours and hours of the girl's evidence, which was lie after lie after lie. It was one protracted plea for sympathy. There were many mentions of her suicidal thoughts but no real descriptions or dates, it was all very vague, and she stuck to her one repeated answer. It was all just fantasy, she was making the whole thing up for kicks, for fun, *just coz lol*. The reason why she had stopped running in the field to look back, she said, was because she wanted to go and help her friend Brianna, she really did, but she was too shocked and she was scared of the boy. But not so shocked and scared not to lie on his behalf to the police in order to protect him. She wanted us to know she was really upset about it all.

Then her cross-examination by the boy's lawyer started, and then again by the CPS. Even in the face of proof that her actions made a mockery of her claims, she lied. At some point she had texted the boy telling him she was good at playing the victim and hiding things. But the evidence had been found and the act was wearing thin. Particularly her claim that she'd been hearing voices. Maybe she thought it would exonerate her? Her post-arrest diagnosis of 'traits of autism' meant that when she was in court she could have a curtain around her so she wasn't 'distracted' by people in the public gallery. That diagnosis has since been rescinded. I didn't buy it at the time, but I also didn't mind; it meant I didn't have to see her. I just hoped and prayed that the jury didn't fall for the act that was going on behind that curtain.

Then we had to go over it all over again for the boy's version of what had happened. He sat in a side room because of his complex special needs and typed his answers. The woman looking after him on remand would read it out to the court over the video link, the barrister would pause, then ask another question. He typed that he heard a puncturing sound like a fizzy drink being opened but didn't see anything from where he was peeing, though he had finally admitted the knife was his and had been used to kill Brianna, but he claimed to have given his fellow defendant his hunting knife when they arrived at the park. She had put it in her waistband while they walked around the park. I knew that Brianna was losing her patience and probably getting cold sitting on the bench waiting for the made-up drug dealer to appear because she sent a friend of hers a text saying she thought the girl she had gone to meet was pretending to be texting a drug dealer. Brianna was not fooled.

'Run, Brianna!' I want to shout. 'Trust your instincts and

run!' Please run. Please start running. The dog-walkers are just coming up the path. You'll be safe. But she didn't run, and the boy alleged that when he reappeared thirty seconds later from behind the trees he saw the girl stab Brianna two or three times. He typed out that he walked over to her to check she was okay. He typed that in his peripheral vision he saw the girl send a text.

Girl: *Why did you ditch us for some random man from Manchester. Like wtf*

It was while checking Brianna, he typed, that he got blood on his hands and face, but then he panicked and followed his friend. She told him to copy her and use his saliva to wash the blood off, which he did. Though both claimed they were victims of circumstance and that they were worried about what the other had done to Brianna, neither were worried enough to stay with the bleeding child in the mud or call 999. No, their instinct was to run, and they were both still running. On 20 December they ran out of road.

'All rise.'

The boy's mother could barely stand up. She was trying to lift herself up by leaning on the table, just to get out of the chair, I felt so sorry for her. My legs were shaking. I held Wes's hands. The foreman announced the verdict.

Guilty is a weighty word. It crushed some people in the court, but for me it brought relief.

'Please take the defendants to the cells.'

The jury had taken just over four and a half hours to come to the decision that the two defendants were jointly responsible for the death of Brianna. It mattered not who had inflicted what injury, all that mattered was that no one believed them that it was a joke gone too far, or just fantasy. They were both murderers and they would be sentenced accordingly.

All around me were the sounds of deep human suffering. Glancing around, I saw so much devastation. I saw the mothers, and they looked like me on the day I had been told my child was dead. Impaled by grief. For what? Why? Why had their children done this? It was inexplicable, and totally pointless. I sat back down, thinking of all the lives they ruined that day. They did it to their families. They did it to my family. They did it to Brianna's friends. And they had done all of this to themselves. Even the jury and everyone who was called to that terrible scene that day. All the investigating officers. And of course to Brianna. Something had to change. She had to not die in vain. I had avoided any public speaking for fear of inadvertently jeopardizing the court case, but I didn't need to stay quiet any more. There was a speech in my pocket. The only question was whether I would be able to say the words. Sometimes the grief snagged the words like fishhooks in my throat, but standing on the steps of the courtroom I was determined to speak from my heart.

'To know how scared my usually fearless child must have been when she was alone in that park with someone she called her friend will haunt me forever . . .'

I wanted to thank everyone, which I managed, and I wanted to reiterate the horrific and terrible loss of my precious child, but lastly I asked for some empathy and compassion for the families of the young people convicted of this horrific crime.

'They too have lost a child,' I said. 'And they must live the rest of their lives knowing what their child has done.'

I knew how people could be, especially online. Only two people had wielded a knife, and it wasn't any of their parents. At what age do we stop blaming parents, anyway? Those kids knew what they were doing. Blame them, as the jury had, not their families, or the school, or the mental health services. In fact, the only thing, I believed then and I believe now, that could have stopped those two from killing Brianna in the park that day was if their plan had been intercepted rather than encrypted, and if I could help make that change, then her death would not be pointless.

I asked for space, to heal, but I promised the press pack, myself, and Brianna, that I would come back in January and fight for that change.

16

Debate, Not Hate

Although I made a promise that I would campaign for a safer world for children, the truth is that it takes its toll. Before every interview I do, there is the torturous ordeal of sitting through the 'reminder' of what led to this point. After every interview I do, the online bullying begins. People argue that it is freedom of speech, but I believe only a tiny handful of people would speak those words of hate to my face. I wanted to find a new approach to promote better mental health for children, but through my experience with Brianna and the conversations I was now having, I soon realized that mindfulness in schools alone could not protect our children. Their wellbeing and development have been pitted against the development of fast-changing technology, and the many messages I received from parents whose kids are struggling, told me we were losing. I was invited to join a campaign group that no one in the group would have chosen to belong to. The Bereaved Families for Online Safety group had been demanding change long before I was added to their membership, and on the eve of Brianna's killers' trial I watched them stand side by side in the House of Lords as the Online Safety Act became law. For five long years, alongside numerous charities, lobbyists, survivors and parliamentarians, they had kept the pressure up, and they had finally won. I am sure they were pleased, but I understood why they were not triumphant. During those years there had been an 82 per cent rise in online grooming and a 66 per cent increase in child abuse image crimes, and why it had taken so very long for the law to respond is a question that has never been satisfactorily answered. I now personally understood that no gain could replace what had been lost. Gains make the loss more bearable. Sometimes.

For another reason, campaigning is a very challenging double-edged sword. I want to keep up the pressure on the tech companies to make the world safer, but to do that I have to use the very technology that I believe contributed to Brianna's declining mental health and her killers' ability to consume content that promotes extreme violence. I want to debate how we build empathy, unity and mental resilience into our schools to help protect children and wider society, but this inevitably opens me up to the abusive onslaught of the dreaded comments page. Comments pages are rarely where constructive debate happens. They're where hate happens. When the hateful comments come in – and I have seen some terrible ones – it is mind-boggling and soul-crushing. A few days after trolling became a crime, and just as the murder trial commenced, I received a message on Facebook.

Your son died because you failed him. You're a failure.

I passed it on to my family liaison officer, who agreed to take it further. The police requested the person's information from Facebook, but the request was rejected due to privacy laws. I was on my knees at the time, coming to terms with witness statements and autopsy reports, but it struck me, even then, that protection ought to go both ways, and currently it does not. Currently a person has the protected right to anonymously call another person 'it', regardless of the harm that word inflicts, but I am not protected from that harm. The words always hurt, but they are not fatal wounds. Unlike my child, I can choose to get back up and fight. Although, during that first terrible year, I am not sure I truly had a choice. I had to get back up and fight or I feared this pain would kill me too.

The first big interview I did after the trial and just before sentencing was on 24 January, on *Good Morning Britain*.

'Has justice been done?' It was hard to sit on that sofa and listen to words like *traumatic, senseless, frenzied, ferocious, brutally stabbed* and *left to die by children with a desire to kill*, and then talk about justice. But I forced myself to speak. Having Brianna back at home with me would be justice, I told them, but since that was never going to happen, campaigning was the closest thing I could come to closure. I

was asked about how it was that I could find compassion
for the families of the convicted children who were await-
ing sentencing. That was an easier question to answer, but
it didn't stop me getting emotional. I told Ed Balls and
Susanna Reid that I had seen myself in the faces of the
mothers when the guilty verdict was read out. How could
I ask for compassion and empathy from others, if I wasn't
able to offer that to the families? I felt I needed to be the
change I wanted to see. And anyway, I had made a promise
to my child, and that kept me going.

'Nobody wants their child to commit such a crime; they
don't need reminding. They know.'

I explained the Peace & Mind campaign and how close
we were to raising enough money to train a mindfulness
teacher for every school in Warrington. But I wasn't going
to stop there, I told them. I had bigger plans.

Things moved at a staggering pace. On 29 January,
Warrington Business Park cemented their support for the
campaign by offering me an official workspace, rent free
for a year. I was shown the office that would become the
headquarters of the Peace & Mind Community Interest
Company. I was so bowled over I cried. Angels, all. Literally.
The purpose of the company is to plant seeds of resilience, empathy and unity, and all the profits go back into
the community. Two days later we hit our Peace & Mind
target and I had meetings with Charlotte Nichols, MP for
Warrington North, and Liz Williams, the woman who had

got mindfulness on to the Welsh curriculum, about how we could push this idea out into the wider world.

I had first met Charlotte Nichols back in August 2023. From the beginning, she had been so unbelievably supportive towards me and my family and had been working alongside the then shadow minister responsible for mental health for a while. We discussed a lot of things, and emails bounced back and forth between us; however, once the court case was over, I had a new focus. Her advice and drive were invaluable, and it was she who suggested raising an adjournment debate in the Houses of Parliament about not only following the Welsh Parliament and getting mindfulness on to our school curriculum but going one step further and creating a module to be embedded in the PGCE teacher-training course. We agreed it might help reduce teacher burnout, which was another pressing issue. She and I would work on the wording, and when the day came, she invited me down to London to hear the discussion in Westminster. Outside, the cherry blossom had started to bloom.

It was just the boost I needed, because the very next day my family and friends walked back into court for the sentencing of Girl X and Boy Y. It was 2 February, nearly a year after they had killed Brianna, and they were going to find out what it had cost them in real time. I knew the press restrictions were going to be lifted on their identities, and I was pleased; in fact, I had advocated for it when I was asked how I felt. Their names would have been released when they were eighteen anyway, and all the gruesome, vicious facts would be dragged up again. I didn't want that. I was relieved they were going to be locked up, but I also wanted them to be shut down. Don't let either of them become beacons, I begged. Instead, I hoped we could erase that negativity and do something positive in its place. Maybe actively building empathy, unity and resilience in the next generation would mean no one felt so powerless in their life that ruining or taking someone else's life became something to aspire to. *Empathy, unity, resilience*, I repeated to myself, over and over, as I took my seat.

I had admired Judge Yip during the trial and I felt confident she had the measure of the two perpetrators. I was glad it was nearly over, but I was dreading it too. Up until sentencing, we had been in the public gallery and I had made a conscious decision not to look at either of the guilty parties. Now we were all in the same room. I didn't want to see their faces, or look directly at them, or watch their reactions, so I kept my focus on the judge, even though some of her words sent shivers through me. She explained that the tariff was life with a minimum time set before each of them could be eligible for parole. That did not determine how long either of them would spend in prison; it could be far, far longer, depending on whether they still presented as a danger to society. The judge made it clear they may never be released. Their families were looking at their sixteen-year-old children and hearing that they might never be released. The minimum time served was set after the age of the prisoner and the severity of their crime had been carefully considered and Judge Yip would now explain her conclusions. This part was hard. I heard the words *sadistic* and *a deep desire to kill*, it was brutal and in part motivated by hostility, but they were young and needed to believe they could be rehabilitated. It was premeditated, yes, but the planning was childish. Each point meant the tariff went up and then down, up and down, up and down . . . It was a forty-minute roller coaster, after the four-week roller coaster of the trial and the four-hour wait for the verdict. No wonder I felt sick most of the time. And then finally, to the girl . . .

'For the murder of Brianna Ghey, you will be detained at His Majesty's pleasure and I set the minimum term of twenty-two years.' To the boy, twenty. He will be thirty-six years old when he gets out, I thought, but whether he would have less hate in his heart for gay or trans people, it was impossible to know. Hopefully, twenty years from now he will have more acceptance in his heart for people who are different to him. My friend, the trans activist and motivational speaker Jaxon Feeley, says the world treats trans people the way the world treated gay people thirty years ago. Twenty years from now, Brianna would have been approaching her thirty-eighth birthday. I wonder what she would have been like at thirty-eight. That is the same age the girl who killed Brianna would be when she is released, if she is deemed no longer a danger to society. I am sorry to say that currently I don't think it is likely she will ever be coming out. I am not sure how you rehabilitate someone who killed for fun, is obsessed with murder and torture and has consistently lied to every professional who has been put in charge of assessing and helping her. She has shown absolutely no remorse, and more than that, has changed her story several times possibly to portray herself in an increasingly malevolent way. A search of her room in the youth offenders' unit discovered a new kill list. On it were the names of some of the people who are there to help her. I was glad when the girl and boy were taken down to the cells and locked up, but my heart was still heavy. As I said, you can win and still never feel victorious.

The girl's family issued a statement. 'All our thoughts are for Brianna and her family. The last twelve months have been beyond our worst nightmares as we have come to real-ize the brutal truth of our daughter's actions. We agree with the jury's verdict, the judge's sentence and the decision to name the culprits.' That is an unbelievably brave and power-ful statement. They thanked me and apologized to everyone affected. Their lives were in turmoil, the lawyer read, but most importantly they wanted to avoid doing anything against our wishes. I knew they were truly sorry because I knew what they were going to say before the statement was made. The family had approached us through Tom

Bedworth, the journalist who had held my hand through so much of this soul-crushing process. The girl's uncle on her maternal side had reached out to him first, to thank us for calling for compassion and empathy after the trial ended. They had been dealing with their own daily doses of internet trolling and vicious vitriol since their daughter had been arrested, and they have since told me that my words had an almost immediate impact. I am glad for that. Of course, it didn't make all the shit go away, but it reduced the flood of abuse they received to a navigable stream, and for that reason they wanted to make sure they returned the favour. They did not want their words to upset us and so found a way for us to hear them before they were read out. I had been mulling over a thought, which was that if I was ever asked about either of the statements issued after court, I would take that opportunity to publicly reach out to the girl's mother, as she had to me. By talking directly to camera, I could communicate two things. Firstly, I did not blame her for her daughter's actions, and secondly, I would be open to meeting her. People might think that mad, but I saw the other mothers in court and felt their pain.

When I got home from the sentencing I was emotionally wrung out and physically shattered, but then I remembered I had a government petition to launch. It was the MP Charlotte Nichols who suggested I start a gov.uk petition, because she was one of the few people who knew I was going to be a guest on *Sunday with Laura Kuenssberg* two days later. I had agreed but, as usual, I had said yes without a clue about what I was saying yes to or how I was going to do it. I really tried, but I found the website hard to negotiate in my exhausted state. Instead, I registered the petition on Change.org, putting together a paragraph about what I was asking for, then sent it into the electronic ether and crashed into bed.

> This petition is born out of a personal tragedy. On February 11, 2023, my daughter Brianna Ghey lost her life in an incident that was planned using the internet. Her killers had easy access to harmful content online, including the 'dark web', where they watched disturbing videos. In addition to this, during her lifetime, Brianna herself struggled with mental health issues and was secretly accessing pro-anorexia and self-harm sites on her smartphone.
>
> This story is a stark reminder of the dangers that unrestricted technology use can pose to our children. It's not just about physical harm; it's also about psychological impact. The internet is filled with harmful content that can easily be accessed by children without meaningful safeguards in place.
>
> We urge mobile phone companies to take responsibility for safeguarding children against such risks associated with technology use. We propose an age limit for smartphone usage and stricter controls over access to social media apps and unsupervised internet use.

The Government says the Online Safety Act protects children, but I don't think it goes far enough.

According to Ofcom, 49 per cent of 8–11-year-olds have a smartphone. This early exposure can lead them into dangerous territories online if left unchecked. Smartphone use in young people has also been shown to impact mood, increasing the risk of depression and anxiety.

It's time we protect our children from these potential harms in their digital lives. We ask you – parents, educators, concerned citizens – to join us in urging mobile phone companies to implement these changes for the safety of our children and future children.

The following day, Tom Bedworth and I boarded a plane to London – all the trains were cancelled. It took forever and felt like a hurdle I could not cope with. That was how wrung out and exhausted I was. To be honest, I don't know how I was still managing to put one foot in front of the other. I went to Broadcasting House in central London to pre-record the interview with Laura Kuenssberg to be aired the following day, Sunday 4 February. We had met before – in the Engine Rooms, of course – and she had offered to assist me with starting a conversation about making phones safer for children. By now it had been well reported that Brianna had issues with anxiety. She may have been manicured and made-up online, but she was, as many teenagers are, insecure about how she looked. I am sure people watching found her inspirational, but there would never be enough 'likes' to assuage the self-doubt. I told Laura Kuenssberg I wanted to see the mobile phone companies take more responsibility for the products they sold because, as I and the parents of the murderers knew from bitter experience, it was almost impossible to keep on top of what our children were doing online. We had that in common.

I had tried to get one Facebook account to take responsibility for one post, and my attempt was shut down. How was Facebook going to moderate hate speech, stop the spread of misinformation and catch groups inciting violence against other groups among their 3 billion people on their platform? They can't. Firstly they don't moderate many of the world's languages and regional dialects and secondly they don't have enough moderators. Mark Zuckerberg had just faced bereaved parents in the US Senate holding up pictures of their dead children and a senator had told the tech bosses they had blood on their hands. If that was true, how many billions of dollars of investment would it take to wipe that blood clean? Perhaps they could put their considerable wealth and innovation into cleaning up their act before any more was spilled? The more I knew, the more I wanted to change.

Tom and I stayed over in London and watched the whole programme live from the studio's viewing gallery. Andrea Thompson, the editor-in-chief of *Marie Claire*, was on the panel and readily agreed with what I was calling for. She knew from the many people who contacted the magazine that the lack of regulation meant parents were struggling to cope. She added that most people understood kids were gorging themselves on the diet of extreme content they were constantly being served. She said that the tech companies knew extreme content got more engagement and it was therefore pushed to the top of the feed, where it got even more engagement, which meant it stayed at the top. First hook them on, then reel them in, and then, most importantly, keep them on the line. While kids are online, the tech companies use AI to sweep and monitor them, not to keep them safe but to mine their information like we once mined coal. Children are the raw materials, and it is a dirty business.

At a magazine, Andrea explained, there are rules and regulations that have to be adhered to, but these did not apply to social media and networks. Those platforms can hide behind their own interpretation of who is a publisher and therefore responsible for content and who is not. Facebook. Snapchat. Twitter, now known as X. 4Chan. Telegram. Twitch. Discord. YouTube. These are not publishers, and they can therefore claim they are not responsible. While that may be true legally, I believe they are at least morally responsible for the content on their platforms. What they absolutely are responsible for is the 'attention economy' – or the destruction-of-attention economy. Tech companies have knowingly created this and fiercely compete with one another for our attention. Their goal is to get our eyeballs fixed to the screen for as long as possible. Profit is all; health and wellbeing be damned. If that wasn't the case, then they would have done something about the harm their products cause, which their own research has revealed. Back in the 1950s, British American Tobacco sat on research that their products – cigarettes – were causing cancer. Instead, they marketed cigarettes to the world as a way to calm the nerves and look mighty fine while doing it. Health be damned.

The 'hook on, reel in and hold fast' design is possibly an even greater threat to children, and while I write – on what would have been Brianna's eighteenth birthday – it is deemed neither harmful nor illegal. The World Health Organization says that children under the age of sixteen should be looking at a screen for no more than two hours a day. Even in that imagined two-hours-a-day utopia, that is fifteen hours a week when kids could be doing something more productive. There was a big news headline recently about how that wasted time could be replaced by a part-time job, and that is true, but they could also be talking to one another, playing, exercising, cooking, reading . . . So it isn't just what they are doing and seeing online that is harmful, it is what being online means they are *no longer* doing.

A recent piece of research by the Japan-based Tohoku Medical Megabank studied over 7,000 babies who were exposed to up to four hours a day of screentime. It concluded that not only was communication and problemsolving negatively affected up to three years later, their fine motor skills were consistently sub-par and their facial muscles were underdeveloped. Before lockdown, my child was high energy, always outside, extremely chatty and a gymnastics obsessive. After lockdown, she was anxious, reclusive and uncommunicative. I said in my victim impact statement that sometimes I feel I lost two children. I realize now I had my first child taken from me by a chronic smartphone addiction, and then I had Brianna taken from me too. I really do mourn them both. The addiction to her phone did not kill Brianna, and I would never imply that it did, but it made the last few years of her life miserable and lonely, and it drove a terrible touchscreen glass barrier between us. I wish I had known then what I know now and what I desperately want others to know before anyone else learns the hard way. The Bereaved Families don't want anyone else joining our group.

Also on the programme that Sunday morning, the former Education Secretary Justine Greening told Laura Kuenssberg that social media and social networking sites had left a long trail of harm and that a lot could be done by simply tightening up rules around age verification, which were, laughably, self-set. I agree with her. About half of eight- to twelve-year-olds admitted to faking their age when they signed up to Instagram, TikTok and Snapchat, and even though their behaviour online reflected their real age – as demonstrated by the genuinely age-appropriate adverts pushed to their devices through the social media accounts – the very same social media companies allowed these underaged children to stay on their platforms. Age verification has subsequently been added to my long list of bugbears. Firstly, why was thirteen deemed safe for children to be left unaccompanied on the internet? The truth is, thirteen was picked for one simple reason. That is the age at which data protection laws decided that children were old enough to sign over rights to a company so they could collect, store and sell on personal information without parental permission. But set by who and based on what research? I would really like to know.

'We wouldn't let a kid go in and buy a porn mag,' said Justine Greening, yet immeasurable numbers of children have seen hardcore porn online. Films are screened and given age-appropriate certificates for the cinema. We don't let seven-year-olds wander in to watch an 18-rated slasher movie, yet immeasurable numbers of children have seen extreme violence on their phones. Even the ones who don't have a smartphone themselves.

This was the case for the ten-year-old daughter of the woman who started the Delay Smartphones campaign. A boy simply leaned over in the choir stall and showed Hannah Oertel's daughter a video of a man being beheaded, an image she could never unsee. For Hannah, it was the final straw. As a therapist, she had seen increasing numbers of young clients presenting with severe anxiety and suffering with fixated negative thinking. Often these thoughts related to a personal comment made online about how they looked. She decided enough was enough and went into campaigning full time. I have also met the parents of Olly Stephens, who have joined an anti-knife campaign and have made documentaries about the link between social media and violent 'peer-on-peer' crime. Their son Olly went to meet a girl in a park. In fact, she had lured him there to be ambushed by two other children who wanted to teach him a lesson for trying to stop them from publicly humiliating a younger boy on Snapchat. Another charming social media invention called 'patterning'. Olly was only thirteen. His killers were thirteen and fourteen, and they plotted their crime on Snapchat. That isn't even Olly's parents' main concern. What really bothers Amanda and Stuart is that if you set up a social media account when you are thirteen, which Olly was, search up interest in sport, popular music and gaming – all of which Olly liked – within hours that profile will be recommended sites 'showing off knives, knives for sale and videos glorifying violence'. Children don't have a chance.

A brilliant short film was made by the *Financial Times* called *Capture: Who's Looking after the Children?*, and the Stephens have helped to get schools to show it to parents. It is worth a watch. There is a caption at the end: *There are fewer regulations protecting children online than there are for the sale of eggs* (Source: FT research). I guess tech companies have more power than poultry farmers.

'The creep over time has muddied our clarity,' said Justine Greening that Sunday morning. Well, I can see that clearly now. 'If the tech is hard to regulate, maybe the safest way is to say: up to sixteen, smartphones should be banned. No one likes banning things, but if a parent thinks they can't keep their kids safe, the government should step in.' The more I know, the more I agree. Nine out of ten kids will by the age of eleven have a device in their pocket that no child, parent or PSHE class can make safe, so that safety needs to be built in.

The person I was really interested in hearing from that morning was Richard Allan, a former Facebook executive and now Liberal Democrat peer. He said that people inside the tech giants are building and advocating for the equivalent of digital seatbelts and airbags, but their voices were quieter than those who wanted to make the cars faster and shinier. You and I – and every consumer – can help redress the balance by refusing to purchase products that are not safe. The Facebook whistleblower Frances Haugen decided to go public when the Civic Integrity arm of Facebook was dissolved after the 2020 US election. But a series of concerns had been building long before that. She saw the internal research which proved that Instagram (owned by Meta) was particularly 'toxic' to teenage girls around the world. There were emails from Nick Clegg to Mark Zuckerberg. Our former Deputy Prime Minister turned Meta President of Global Affairs was asking for more resources to clean up Facebook, but he was turned down. I have subsequently spoken to another Facebook whistleblower who claims that Meta could alter the way information is disseminated and distributed to young people overnight, and I have no reason to disbelieve him. If Facebook knows before you do that you are going to split up with your partner, leave your job, have plastic surgery, buy a dog – then they are either reading your thoughts or, worse still, placing them there.

One thing is now clear to me: the time for self-regulation within the tech industry is over. They have been marking their own homework for too long and have been caught cheating. The US is far away from creating an Online Safety Act, and tech companies operate all over the world, however, we should be proud that the UK, a big and wealthy market, has at least started to make the online world a safer place for children. Thanks to our Online Safety Act, there are several laborious things companies have to do if they want to continue to sell to children. This essential Act of Parliament is beginning to take affect because in the UK at least, if companies don't comply, they either have to leave the UK market or they have to get their act together. As a result, Meta have introduced Teen Accounts on Instagram and ByteDance have announced that TikTok will ban certain filters for certain ages. Makes you realize what they can do but only when they have to.

Listening to the discussion between Peter Allan and Laura Kuenssberg, I had a sudden memory of playing a game on Roblox in which I could hear children laughing, which I found very disturbing. There is no barrier to entry. Any other adult could have been listening to these children, could message them directly and say whatever they wanted to them. It was horrendous and with a finely tuned malevolent eye, anyone could pick out the vulnerable kid, the one always online, compliment them, befriend them and then casually drop in the possibility of exchanging direct message handles like Snapchat or WhatsApp to be able to chat more easily, and with even fewer eyes on. And that, ladies and gentlemen, is how grooming and exploitation begins. Roblox hosts countless consumer-created games for children to play and every day more are added. That could be finding jewels in a field of flowers, discovering spells in a magical forest, watching a gang rape in a strip joint or, like Hotline, perform a task where players get to knock each other over with knives then beat each other's heads in until they die with blood splatters.

Dangerous games aren't all we have to worry about. Live beamed from USA, Peter Kyle, now Secretary of State for Science, Innovation and Technology, listed all the new issues facing children to Laura Kuenssberg. The one that jumped out at me for obvious reasons was the pathway from social media into the Dark Web and how children are being funnelled in that direction. I know that the children who plotted and killed my child had searched up and shared dangerous and violent content on the internet. When she got bored with what Netflix had to offer, the girl had searched up and found true crime, then, when that wasn't enough, she searched up crimes that were not being re-enacted, they were actually taking place. Fantasy ceases to be fantastical when it has been realized, so when that wasn't enough, she was able to download an APP, a TOR browser that gave her access to the Dark Web. Once that has happened, there is very little any parent can do to stop their child accessing material so warped it has the power to warp a mind. It should not have been possible for the girl, aged fourteen at the time, to put that software on her phone. And as for monitoring your child's phone, I know from experience how hard it is. Brianna punched holes in the walls when I tried to check hers, so is it too much for parents to ask for some help? Peter Kyle was offering to make a strategic statement to Ofcom which would force it to prioritize certain issues so that harm could be mitigated before it happens. AI, chatbots, deepfakes – these were all on the horizon and were a clear and present danger to young and vulnerable people. Not to mention grooming and the rise of extremism. So it isn't hard to imagine that I was pretty revved up by the time I met all the other guests after the show. Perhaps it was the early start, or that I was missing home, but when Gillian Keegan, then Secretary of State for Education, gave me the 'look what we've done: passing the OSA' statement followed by the 'let's wait and see if it works' argument about whether we needed to go further and ban smartphones in schools, delay smartphones for children and introduce mindfulness to the curriculum, it just wound me up. Laura Kuenssberg could not have been more accurate when she said I wanted to turn my agony into action. Action was the key word for me. I didn't feel like listening to people talking about what could be done, rather than doing what they talked about.

'That's not enough,' I replied rather abruptly to the Secretary of State for Education. I think Tom was taken aback. He'd never seen me disagree with or question anyone in authority, but as I said, I was getting a little tired of talk. That very personal attack online telling me that I had failed my child sat heavy in my heart. That's the trouble with nasty comments – they worm their way into your psyche and take root. Laura said no one listening to me would feel I had failed Brianna. But I did fail her. I was all she had to protect her against all this horror, and I had failed to keep her safe. As I travelled back to Warrington to face the first anniversary of her death, I vowed that I would not fail her again.

17

Don't Get High on
Your Own Supply

Anniversaries are painful. I genuinely didn't think I would be able to stand at the one-year memorial vigil on 11 February 2024 in Golden Square, Warrington, let alone speak. Brianna's friends had been so brave, and I really wanted to acknowledge that seeing all those people, standing united, made a real difference to me. Every single person there, stranger or friend, helped me remember the good times. They allowed me to be grateful for who Brianna was, and for the sixteen years we had with her. My strength came from the people looking back at me. So I wrapped myself up in my protective pink coat and walked to the mic.

'I will be forever thankful that I was lucky enough to spend sixteen years with Brianna. She taught me so much and gave me so much happiness and love. If there is one piece of advice I can give to any parent, it would be to hug your children tight and never stop telling them that you love them.'

Those last words reflect one of my deepest regrets, and yet I was aware that by coming together to celebrate

Brianna's life we had created something that felt a lot like love.

If I was going to get through this, I had to build on that love, for myself as much as for the people around me, which is why I was genuinely pleased that my invitation to meet the mother of Girl X was accepted. For a year, she'd not been to a shop locally and, like me, had taken her dog far away to walk for hours and hours, torturing herself about what she might have – *must have* – missed. During the trial, she later told me, she'd not been able to even look at me, so terribly guilty did she feel, so to come to Birchwood to meet me face to face showed true courage. I think our first act of comradeship was us both believing, in a certain way, that the other was having a harder time. I knew I was grieving, mourning a loss I would never recover from, but could hopefully, in time, find a way to live with. And I understood that she, too, was grieving and mourning a loss she would never recover from, but it was one she would never be able to live with. How could she? She, on the other hand, felt that at least her child – being still alive – might have another chance, whereas mine did not, and that's why she thought it was a million times worse for me. It was within that compassion for the other person that we both found common ground.

We fell into each other's arms and sobbed. Though I was nervous, and I am sure she was petrified, we found we had a lot to talk about and I could see in her a mirror of my own deep sadness. Quickly we started talking about how hard it was to parent a child when you were competing with a phone, and very soon we found we were, again, on common ground. Both of us had been shocked and traumatized by the material we discovered our children had been able to access yet effectively hide. Both of us had to come to terms with the fact that our lives had been irreversibly destroyed. Neither of us could go back to the jobs we had loved. Her brother has been a rock to her, as Wes has been to me, and he said to her early on and I absolutely agree, 'Don't try to understand this. Better to come to terms with the fact that this will never, ever make sense.' Trying to understand what happened, and why, would mean revisiting Culcheth Linear Park, and I personally never want to go back there, spiritually, mentally or physically, because that would break me. The child she heard about in court was not the child she had known at home and is not the child she visits weekly. Her brother also said to her, 'Take one day at a time.' She and I are both still doing that. I know some of her friends find our friendship – which is what it has become – macabre, but if our families can find unity out of this horror, then maybe there is hope for the tribalism that seems to be blighting the modern world.

Soon after that first meeting, she and I started to have coffee once a week. It helped me to be with someone who understood on a molecular level what I was feeling. When I started the Community Interest Company, she offered to help in whatever way she could. Like me, she has good days and bad days; like me, she finds doing something positive is helpful; like me, there are days when she feels it is too much and when her friends and family reach down and pull her up. She and her son gave their time and energy to our first Peace Festival, which took place on my birthday, 15 September 2024, a year after we'd launched the Peace & Mind campaign to get mindfulness into schools. Another first anniversary full of mixed feelings. So much had happened because of Brianna, but *without* Brianna. I was another year older. Brianna was still sixteen.

I was taken aback by the overwhelming support for the idea from teachers and parents; we had managed to raise almost £84,000. I am delighted to report that at least one eager teacher from almost every school in Warrington has enrolled in the training, which is being delivered by the Mindfulness in Schools Project. I feel ever more passionate about this because I know how much mindfulness helped me build the high level of mental resilience I needed to get through the heartbreaking 'year of firsts' without Brianna. And the much-needed self-compassion, so that my sense of personal failure didn't take me to such terrible depths I could not climb out. And lastly, the ability to feel empathy towards others. In doing so, mindfulness has had the power to dissolve a barrier between prosecution and defence, only for us to discover we are in fact on the same side. We just want our carefree children back.

It is this knowledge that makes me want to share the fundamental building blocks for inner strength and mental resilience, but I also have a new understanding of how difficult that can be. For quite a long time after Brianna died, I managed to carry on with my mindfulness routine, finding moments on those long walks away from Warrington to find awe in nature. But, full disclosure, I am definitely not in that routine right now. Frankly, right now I feel like I'm struggling to find the time to . . . well, you can imagine the rest of that sentence. I have tried to get back into it but have consistently failed to find even five minutes to stop and breathe and take stock and focus. Instead, I feel like I am in a washing machine that is stuck on a fast cycle. It's not good, and I know it's not good, but I can't seem to get out of the washing machine. My closest friends might hint that instead of getting out I keep clicking the programme and adding more load . . . and maybe they have a point.

Tap, tap, tap go those nails.

Okay, they do have a point, but in a way it's been good to be reminded that sometimes – usually when you need it most – practising mindfulness can be challenging. I feel I don't have the time or the energy to sit and shut my eyes for a few minutes, which is a stark but timely reminder that practising mindfulness is not always easy. So when I bang on about mindfulness, which I know I do, I am really saying, just start thinking about it. Start small. Practising mindfulness is more like taking up a fitness routine, like resistance training for the mind. You start with a small, easy handheld weight and gradually build up strength over time. Like most exercise routines, you get into it and then you fall out of it and then you get into it and then you fall out of it, but the muscle memory is there every time you go back. Luckily, I seem to have a guardian angel, because a year after I was first offered the mindfulness training by MiSP, which back then I wasn't in a fit state to do, it has arrived. A year ago, I was too traumatized and there was too much going on with the trial to sit and be in the moment, because the moment was too awful. Focusing on my feelings felt counterproductive. My feelings could become monstrous and turn on me, so I am deeply grateful that the training opportunity has come now because the weekly sessions will help me get back into practising this vital skill, hold me safe and keep me accountable, even if it is just for a few seconds at a time.

I was glad I already had eight years of practice behind me because when our world went dark it meant I was able to find chinks of light that guided me to where I am now. I am thankful to have the practice back in my life and I am thankful for the wonderful people it has brought me. My grief is my own, but I am not alone. Connections create a safety net, and I could not continue along this tightrope walk without knowing they are there to catch me when I fall. That is what working with MiSP has given me, so please, forgive me while I just stand on my soap box for a few more minutes. Mindfulness is not just about stopping to look at the daisies, it's about what stopping to look at the daisies is doing for you. It helps to train your attention so you become more aware of what's happening in the present moment, rather than worrying about the past or the future. That awareness helps you to better understand your feelings. When you are able to recognize your feelings, you can develop an understanding about what is making you feel a certain way. When you know yourself better, you can make better lifestyle choices. Think of it as mental upcycling. Each time there is a fearful or negative thought, you learn to notice it, accept it, then let it go. In that way we can resist the downward spiral of negative thinking – and this links me right back to the subject of online safety for children, which is vital, because research has shown that access to harmful online content ignites negative thinking. As I wrote to Sir Keir Starmer after he became our Prime Minister, I believe mindfulness techniques support well-being by improving resilience, anxiety, focus, retention and recall of information, flexibility, friendships and emotions. If we are to realize the full potential of this life-changing project, we need government support.

That's the thing about anniversaries: they remind me of how far we have come, but also how far we still have to go. We've left our children defenceless in a corrupting digital world, and in case anyone is still in any doubt, it should be noted that more children and young people than ever before are struggling with their mental health. The number of school-age children being referred to CAMHS has risen by 76 per cent since 2019, escalating to over 1.4 million in 2022, according to NHS figures. Anxiety disorders are estimated to affect 5–19 per cent of all children and adolescents in the UK, and about 2–5 per cent of children under the age of twelve. The knock-on effect is real. Almost 80 per cent of teachers now report experiencing stress at work, due to factors such as increasing workload and rising and unrealistic expectations, with over 35 per cent reporting that they had experienced 'burnout' and over 50 per cent insomnia or difficulty sleeping. Not to mention the burnout within the mental health services, people who are doing their best but who are trying to put out a raging furnace with an ice lolly. Schools can't fix this. Parents can't fix this. Mental health practitioners can't fix this. Only tech companies and government can fix this, but we can help our children by building up their defences, and our awareness, while we wait for the tech companies to do the right thing and change the way they do business.

The other anniversary we have 'celebrated' is the passing of the Online Safety Act (OSA). Again, it was a huge achievement to get the bill passed, but we have more to do. The Bereaved Families are still calling for ministers to urgently commit to a new bill that strengthens regulation. They've been busy polling, and the research reflects the conversations I am constantly having with people and the anecdotal stories I am told. Four in five parents think politicians should be tightening the rules, while three in four think the previous government was too slow to introduce regulation. Again, I would really like to know why they held off. 'Timidity will cost lives,' said Ian Russell, seven years after his precious daughter Molly was served up so much graphic, pro-suicidal content which romanticized acts of self-harm and further isolated her by actively discouraging her from talking to her parents that the coroner found the social media sites she followed contributed to her death. His report to prevent future deaths was sent to Pinterest, Meta, Snap Inc and X.

If we clamour loud enough, then hopefully I won't be saying the same thing seven years from now and Ofcom will have finalized the illegal harms code and risk assessment guidance that will ensure that providers take responsibility for ensuring their products are safe for their users *before* they go to market. This is not the case as I write, but – if we hold them to account – should be in place by 2025.

The US Centers for Disease Control and Prevention reports the average daily hours spent on a screen by age group: 8–10 years, six hours; 11–14 years, a staggering nine hours; and 15–18 years, seven and a half hours. At the risk of repeating myself, remember the World Health Organization recommendation for 5–17-year-olds is no more than two hours a day. *Two hours a day!* From lockdown onwards, Brianna was on her phone every waking hour, and those hours got longer the less she slept. It is now well documented that excessive screen time by young people is linked to obesity, depression, behavioural issues, anxiety, insomnia, development of social skills and impatience. Half of parents report that their child's personality altered after being given a smartphone and wish they had held off for longer. I fall into that category. The only thing on that list Brianna did not suffer with is obesity, but she had chronically disordered eating, so I believe she even checks that box. Is it too much to ask for a Green Cross Code-style campaign from the government to educate people on how to take care of their smartphone usage and mental health? We did it for drink-driving, smoking, safe sex, so why not explain the damage of too much screen time? This isn't about creating a nanny state, it's about empowering people with knowledge. The tech companies aren't going to give us safe products until we demand them, but we have to know they aren't safe in the first place, and I'm not sure everyone does.

Nowadays, 5–7-year-olds are increasingly online, with up to a third using social media unsupervised. Many have personal profiles clearly in breach of the age verification barrier. They are accessing high-risk social networks and live-streamed content. Three quarters of children in the same age bracket use a tablet and the numbers are rising year on year so if now is not the time to take action, when will be? And so we have no choice but to keep up the pressure, and community groups like Delay Smartphones, Smartphone Free Childhood, Common Sense Media, Internet Matters and Bereaved Families for Online Safety continue to make irritants of our ourselves. I believe we do this for two main reasons. Firstly, as I have said, in my opinion we have to go further, but secondly, because unless we stay focused on our goal, regulation can get watered down. Even in light of all we know, the House of Lords attempted to weaken the part of the OSA which stipulated that coroners would be able to force tech companies to release information to the parents of the deceased, once again claiming data protection. The Bereaved Families for Online Safety group went into action and was instrumental in reversing that. This gives me hope. Look what we can do when we put our collective minds to it.

I've been having off-the-record conversations with several mobile phone companies for a while now. No phone company can legally sell a smartphone to anyone under eighteen years old, unless it's a PAYG phone, so the only age they have on record is that of the person taking out the contract. I met Mat Sears, the corporate affairs director of EE, and a parent himself, on our podcast Parents vs the Internet, and he told me and Liz Hall that EE is aware that many of their phones end up in the hands of children and the company has become increasingly worried. Having listened to their customers, EE has made the decision to look into updating their guidance and education and has already created something called PhoneSmart in partnership with Internet Matters. This is a little like taking a cycling proficiency test for phones, a way to put some stabilizers on for a while, because EE knows you can't put a smartphone in the hands of a child and expect them to know how to use it safely. EE has gone further, concluding that no amount of education or guidance could make a smartphone safe for anyone under the age of eleven, so they are urging parents not to buy smartphones for children at all. A non-smartphone will do.

They've also declared that for children aged between eleven and thirteen, social media itself makes smartphones unsafe and should categorically not be downloaded. Between thirteen and sixteen years of age, if it is downloaded it should still be monitored – and the tech already exists to do that. A company called Chirp, and another called Sway, make software that can sit on handsets and gently nudge users away from harmful content by suggesting more empowering sites. I admire all this work, but this does require the person using the handset to tell the truth about their age. It is still too easy to fake your age when signing up to any networking or social media app.

I am wary of anything that puts the burden of monitoring on the shoulders of the parents because I know how hard it is. However, I also know we need to know more and trust less; we need to stay interested even if the kids don't like it. I am not alone in saying sometimes this is so hard it breaks the relationship between parent and child, which is why it can't just be on the shoulders of parents. So, until what is or isn't age appropriate is formally identified and linked to safety – like it is for films, cigarettes, driving, gambling, adult content and alcohol – thereby making the need for age-verification tech to become watertight, much of this is ineffective. This is why more pressure is being put on the government to amend the OSA to include rigorous age verification requiring photographic ID. Some have suggested it could go through a secondary process that links the photo ID to an NHS number for children. No doubt some kids will climb any hurdle, but let's put something in their way rather than simply allowing them to scroll through a list of years and click on any one they choose. Some say what is being asked for is too much; some say it is not enough. I say let us find common ground between the tribes and acknowledge that whether we are for the prosecution or the defence, we are in fact on the same side. I think we all just want our carefree children back.

Another group trying to get a handle on the issue of child protection online and on phones is the Better Phone Project, a group of consumers literally asking for a better phone to counter the rise in anxiety and addiction to social media. They are urgently advocating for a handset to be designed which offers inbuilt safety, where slow software upgrades match the age or vulnerability of the user and which don't require the purchase of a new phone. It isn't just parents asking for this, it is young people themselves and carers of vulnerable people. The market is responding. There are Dash Phones, reminiscent of the once-loved Nokia Brick, and the Light Phone, with reviewers happily reporting on the hours they get back each day and the peace of mind that comes from more intentional internet usage. The handset is small and has Paperwhite technology so there is no blue light, which is linked to eye strain and sleeplessness. There is the Balance Phone, designed to – yup, you guessed it – create more balance between time spent online and offline by reducing screen time. Balance phones have no addictive apps or websites – no gambling, no porn, no social media . . . In the States you can buy a Gabb phone which has safety built in and cannot be reversed by canny kids. Talking of canny kids, have you heard about the ones who take their phones out of the recognizable covers, plug in the empty case to 'charge' overnight where the parents can see them, then sneak their phones into their rooms. Just a heads up.

All this innovation is exciting, however it is in battle against the adolescent phone of choice: the Apple iPhone. And Apple has built a handset that, by design, cannot be altered for the user's age or vulnerability. Apple? Are you listening? I know you know, because it is well documented that even Steve Jobs's house was a tech-free zone. He famously didn't allow his children to use iPads or iPhones because he believed too much tech could be addictive.

What's that thing drug dealers say? 'Don't get high on your own supply.'

On that subject, I bet Mark Zuckerberg's three young daughters won't be allowed to lie about their age to go on all their dad's platforms. I'm sure they won't be allowed to doom-scroll through endless short-form videos. Unlike the rest of us, they will have all the latest safeguarding tech available to them and their family has the money to make sure the children are constantly looked after. That's a bit harder for a working single mother. The companies even refer to us as 'users', proudly. TikTok has 1 billion users. YouTube has 2.5 billion active users. Facebook over 3 billion users. Instagram boasts of their 2 billion monthly active users. Elon Musk won't release the figures but has claimed that X has up to 250 million users each day. They want us to use, they push us to use, and they are getting very rich and extremely powerful doing it. Social media is the perfect gateway drug to the hard class-A drugs that ruin lives and kill people. By serving up suicide, anorexia, extremism, self-injury, violent sexual images that fuel murderous fantasy, 24/7 gambling sites, bots that tell you they love you then tell you to die, 'users' become so desensitized that eventually nothing on the surface internet will satisfy. So you download an onion router and start mainlining the hard stuff.

Many other companies make money selling advertising space on these platforms. Between violent beheading videos and porn which glorifies rape there are famous sportswear ads, car ads – companies from around the world have spent a fortune building their brands, only to be stuck between a person brandishing a knife and spouting hate and an incel advocating taking a hammer to one's own face to build up an alpha male 'Chad' look. Between reels selling starvation and sign-off videos selling suicide, there are ads for well-known cosmetics and menstruation products. The companies have no idea where their ads will land. If I was a brand manager at a big corporation, I would have a real problem with that. But the really terrifying thing is that most of this warped content is legal. Protected. Which brings me to my last – well, nearly last – bugbear. Legal but harmful content makes up most of the stuff our kids are viewing and responding to. I know personally what it is like to be on the receiving end of legal but harmful content. When, in July 2024, I took on the campaign to get mindfulness on to the curriculum, I did a lot of press. The double-edged sword I was talking about means putting myself into the lion's den with the aim of taming the beast but protected by nothing more than hope. A clip from my Sky News interview was reposted on their X, formerly Twitter, page. Within seconds, the comments came in . . .

A son by the way who was clearly being groomed online
Is this the mother who bought her son kinky underwear
and put him on tiktok

What about your son
Totally ignores all the good work going on in schools

Then there is a break in the comments for a warning line that the next barrage of comments was 'probable spam' and *may* be considered harmful. I kept thinking as I scrolled down how many of the people posting were unlikely to say any of this to my face.

Bros been dead like 10,000, let him rot
She should take some responsibility.
Sky News why do you encourage mental disorders?
It wasn't her daughter, it was her son.

The Coming of Messiah posted a meme of a banana having the end cut off and a 'It's a Boy!' celebration.
Who sends their son to school dressed as an anime hooker? asked a person with his face obscured by a very unnerving mask. No name, obviously.

Mindfulness should be well down the list of psychiatric
treatments this mother should have received.

It was personal, toxic, hurtful and unhelpful, but all totally legal. I admire the *Guardian* for coming off X – it really is a cesspit. Truth now lies in the hands of a very few unelected tech oligarchs who sow distrust, keep us hooked and shut down anyone who tries to hold them to account.

The trolling floored me, as it had done before. It took

me about a day to recover, then it galvanized me back into action. We needed more compassion, more empathy, more resilience. Without compassion we can't listen, without empathy we can't heal, and without resilience we can't resist the dark place the internet can lure you to.

And we need to be resilient because it is a fast-changing landscape. Just the other day I received an email from a journalist from the *Daily Telegraph* who was investigating Character AI, the online chatbot tool that allows people, including children, to 'talk' to bots that are imitating real people or fictious characters. Alarmingly, there were several where you can 'talk' to Brianna. The most popular one had over 10,000 conversations before it was taken down. Google is investing millions into this new tech, even though it has already been proven it is not safe for children and was rushed to market before any real due diligence was done. Megan Garcia, the mother of an American teenager, is suing the company – naming the now mega-rich former Google employees who invented Character AI in the suit. Her son, Sewell, spent months talking to a bot imitating a popular character from *Game of Thrones*, Daenerys Targaryen. The chats became increasingly sexualized, and Sewell fell in love. 'She' sadly encouraged and then goaded him into suicide. There are 20 million global users who, paying just under £10 a month, can speak one to one with their chatbots. This particular Character AI was taken down, not because the inventor had caused the death of a child, but because they were found to be breaking Intellectual Property law. Daenerys Targaryen – a fictitious character – is protected by copyright. Brianna – a human being – is not.

Brianna isn't the only murdered child who has been resurrected, there is also Drew Crecente, an eighteen-year-old killed by her ex-boyfriend. This product is absolutely not fit for purpose, especially for children, but Google paid $2.7 billion for it and no doubt will be wanting a big return on its investment, so watch out for targeted ads coming to an inbox near you. Sorry if I sound cynical – I *am* cynical, because I know, for certain, that the tech companies, like big food companies, know they are harming their customers. The most recent research says that addictive food is costing this country £286 billion a year; I wonder what addictive tech is costing us?

By the time this book goes to print, no doubt there will be another tech assault taking place on our senses. We will suffer while the inventors and investors will get richer. I want us all to benefit from the digital age, I really do. Is it too much to ask that we make tech safe for children, at the very least? I have heard two former Facebook executives say that the software *already* exists to reduce many dangerous aspects of the online world, but it won't be implemented until it is in Facebook's financial interest to do so. An eighteen-year-old called Barrett Riley drove his father's Tesla into a Tesla garage and asked them to override the parental 'chill mode' control. After this was done, he lost control of the car, driving it into a wall at 113mph in a 30mph area. The battery burst into flames and Barrett and his friend Edgar were killed. A month later, after Barrett's father petitioned Elon Musk himself, there was a software update sent out to all Tesla cars in Barrett Riley's name that meant parents could set speed controls with a PIN which could not be overridden without their permission, code or knowledge. The update took two hours. Which just goes to show that the tech companies can do this, but sadly they only choose to do so when they have the PR nightmare of a dead child haunting their brand. Mr Riley said he would like to 'acknowledge that Barrett and Edgar's loss led to the enhanced safety of others'. I know how he feels, but please, no more dead children.

If we boycott unsafe products, if we refuse to put dangerous handsets into the hands of our children, the makers of those handsets will build better products because, let's be honest, they would want us to start buying again. Until we make them install safeguarding software at the point of purchase, they will continue to sacrifice our health as they fast-track big profits. All products, both Apple and Android, require us to regularly install upgrades, so I know they can retrospectively install important guard-rail software the way they do security fixes. That would protect the millions of children currently at risk on iPhones and iPads. I am sure some people will get very hot under the collar about privacy laws, but we are talking about children here. Children deserve to be protected. And honestly, is there really anything private about the internet? When a child is pressurized into sending a 'self-generated' nude image, that image is likely to be screened and scanned by the National Crime Agency (NCA) because all child pornography is illegal. The NCA is trying to save sexually exploited children from ending up being tortured and sexually assaulted in a 'red room', like the ones Girl X accessed. In the end – and this is the hopeful bit – the power rests with us. I just don't think many of us know it. I am a food technologist by trade. Once upon a time, in a different life, I was responsible for creating new products. When I did the job I loved, I legally had to list every single ingredient in each pie filling I developed. I even had to explain the ingredients in terms understandable to non-food technologists, plus a serving suggestion (i.e. one pie, not the whole pack), and the regulations were rightly particularly stringent around sugar, salt and saturated fat because they are unhealthy, addictive and not good for any of us in any sort of quantity. This is why calories are listed both as a total and according to a set amount, either 100g or 100ml, or a serving suggestion of 30g (beware of those: they can be unrealistically small!). The calories are also listed as a percentage of the average recommended daily intake. Some companies have gone even further and colour-coded the fat, saturated fat, salt and sugar content so that the harmful (but legal) content immediately jumps out at you. Red for high risk, amber for medium, green for low. Can't we make children a healthy, low-risk, non-addictive, green-rated phone? I mean, why shouldn't tech companies be held to the same account as any other industry? After all, we consume vast amounts of their digital fodder, and most of it is junk. I would like to be able to say that Brianna's loss led to enhanced safety for others. Please.

Epilogue

Look Brianna, Look What We Can Do

When I turned twenty-one, my mother gave me a book on Buddhism, which I was too traumatized to read. She was trying to throw me a lifeline and I ignored it because, honestly, deep down, I did not believe I deserved saving. I've read up on Buddhism now and many of the fundamental tenets I've taken into my heart and life, like meditation, mindfulness and yoga. I do not pretend to be an expert Buddhist, but I have personally found aspects helpful, and I would probably be a basket case without them. My amateur understanding of reincarnation is that by living in the present with love and compassion, even amidst suffering, our words and actions in this life create karma for our next. This is not about 'toxic positivity' – where *everything*, however terrible, *happens for a reason* – but about finding a way through the pain when the pain comes, and truly, I don't know anyone who has managed to get through life without some pain. I guess these ideas are the building blocks for many religions and, for obvious reasons, the idea that my child has not gone forever brings me comfort. In addition to my own wellbeing, helping free children from the suffering inflicted by the offline–online continuum we've inadvertently created for them, is the reason I get out of bed in the morning. Even when I don't want to. And I often don't.

When Brianna reached an impressive number of online followers, I mentioned that she could create some good karma and do something positive with her burgeoning platform, something that would feed her soul rather than consume it from the inside. I was trying to throw her a lifeline but she, like me, ignored it. I found notes she'd written to herself after she died – lists reminding herself to do better, be better, work harder, tidy up the mess she'd made. Her internal sense of failure is heavy on the page. In Buddhism and other ancient religions, living souls can be consumed by Hungry Ghosts. They lodge inside us and feed on misery, insecurity and are utterly insatiable. Whatever you feed a hungry ghost is not enough; they remain hungry. I know from personal experience that toxic abusive relationships create hungry ghosts and there are fewer more damaging relationships than the ones our children are having with their phones. I think social media made a hungry ghost of my child. I like to think she would have escaped that toxic relationship in the end; I believe she could have become a great advocate for unity and understanding, and that finding a sense of purpose would have been the making of her.

Clearly, I am no monk, and I don't know how the karma and reincarnation system works, but indirectly I think Brianna has made a difference, and if that isn't enough good karma, I've been working hard in her absence. I know from the pattern of wounds she received when she was attacked, she did not want to die. She put up a fight. I am just trying to continue that fight.

I like to imagine that somewhere in the future everything we have campaigned for has come to pass. Look, Brianna, I want to say to every pink sky I see, look what we can do. And one day I will say: look what we have done.

I'll tell her that the government spent what was needed to roll out the evidence-based mindfulness in schools project, it took time but there was a greater uptake than the estimated 75 per cent of teachers. Now all children are taught the fundamental difference between reaction and response and how to cope with many of their complex feelings. Through basic grounding exercises which keep them anchored in and focused on the present they can choose how to respond to the difficulties life throws at them rather than reacting to them from a place of past angers or future fears. Cases of clinical anxiety and depression have been coming steadily down since their peak in 2025 when consumers decided enough was enough and they would no longer put dangerous digital devices into their children's hands. The tech companies responded quickly and innovatively to the catastrophic drop in sales with such brilliant child-safe tech that adults started clamouring for it too. No more constant buzzing of notifications. 'For You' recommendations are time and content limited. No automatic 'Up Next'. No more doom-scrolling. You choose how you use the internet, rather than the internet using you.

MiSP is being rolled out in the Early Years sector. It is embedded into the teacher-training curriculum too and overall there are more graduates going into this rewarding profession, greater retention and less reported burnout. Teachers teach children how to think, ProfAI does the marking, building a picture of skills and ability, weaknesses and strengths, developed to discover natural talents so children can proceed according to their development and circumstance rather than their year group. These statistics are collected and mapped over time, giving far more accurate and nuanced results to Ofsted about how the children at each school are progressing than the now obsolete surprise inspection. Far fewer children get left behind, because tech is used creatively to match children with appropriate areas of interest. Everyone still has to do maths though! Sorry.

MiSP-trained teachers train more teachers who train more teachers, each paying it forward, guaranteeing that every new influx of children benefits from increased mental resilience. There is no waiting list for children requiring acute mental health services as the combination of safe phone use and brain-training reversed the downward spiral of mental health issues among adolescents, freeing up the services to work with the complex systemic and acute crisis cases that do arise. There are no phones in primary schools at all, however, SENtech is incorporated into the classrooms to level the playing field for children with a variety of challenges. A child with dyslexia, dyspraxia, rapid eye tracking issues, ADHD and ASD can dictate their work on voice recognition tech and AI-generated feedback is taught directly to the child through earphones, reducing the help as the child progresses.

Only child-safe phones are legally sold to secondary school age children between the ages of twelve and sixteen. The two-stage handset is linked to a 'parent' phone as well as the child using unique age-verification codes, fingerprints and biometrics. This means the child can learn to use the tech in the same way they learn to drive. Social media is banned up to the age of sixteen and handsets have built-in protection which means VPNs, apps, onion routers, etc. cannot be uploaded on to the phone itself. The safety features include set time limits of use, flagging up concerning words that a child might be searching for, and the ability to link GPS tracking to the caregiver. Phones, like the Tesla, have a 'lock-out' curfew feature which shuts off the device at a certain time. There is no factory reset, which not only reduces phone theft and digital abuse but stops children over-riding parental controls.

Each secondary school can choose from a variety of systems designed by the government on whether to ban phones on the premises, place phones in electronically sealed bags, or install deactivation or curfew tech on smart phones and within the network. All child-safe phones have SOS buttons linked to Childline, so no child is unable to report abuse of any kind. PREVENT expands its schools programme to include all grooming, not just extremism. 'Talk Relationships' and 'Stop the Hate Before It's Too Late' is included in the secondary school curriculum so children learn to recognize prejudice, toxic behaviour, coercive control and gaslighting inside relationships and families to reduce both perpetrators and victims of peer-on-peer and gender-based violence.

Peace & Mind UK started a referral scheme for primary school age children in Warrington who, like you, struggled. The whole family goes for group mindfulness sessions which are designed to strengthen the bonds between everyone in the family, so they can support themselves and each other. It was such a success they are rolling it out across the country! Teaching has become more tutor-led, focused learning, problem solving and thinking and discussion groups. The removal of smartphones from the school environment frees up hours for community-based sports, gymnastics, dance, drama, art, design, vocational skill building and group craft and practical work, including upcycling, recycling and fixing. It's amazing what the kids do these days, so by the time you reach sixth form – if academics isn't your thing – you can work towards a fully vocational qualification and yes, that includes hair, nails and make-up, textiles and tailoring. There's no uniform by sixth form either. Though skirt lengths remain an issue. Apart from that – you'd love it.

It's safe.

You can come back now.

Postscript

Creative Writing Homework,
Birchwood School, November 2022

Cigarettes and Diet Coke
By Brianna Ghey

All sounds are faded, my eyes are foggy.

'Hanna.'

I flutter my sunken eyes with thick lashes dragging down my bloodshot eyes and look up, it was my friend, Poppy.

'Girl you just totally blanked,' she blabbed.

'I was just thinking,' I mumbled.

She carried on rambling – 'anyways, as I was saying we should literally invite Josh to the party and maybe even . . .' all sounds slowly muffled and blended into one. I look around my stuffy college corridor, people laughing and pushing, I look to the left and the whole place spins. I widen my eyes to focus.

'I'm gonna get a coke,' I stated to the group of girls gossiping.

'Oh, I'll come too!' Poppy said, while obnoxiously nudging the other girls out the way with her skinny hands with long hot pink acrylics to get to me. I smiled and turned to walk to the cafeteria while linking onto her arm but bump into Jake.

'Oh, sorry,' I said in a wobbled voice while nervously chuckling. He smelt like smoke and cheap deodorant spray, his tracksuit was grey and dull I look up to his red tired eyes. We walked around him and his friends, Poppy looked at me with a confused face while smiling, I giggled and rolled my eyes.

I investigate the refrigerated shelves for a diet coke, I pick up the overpriced, refreshing-cold drink and grabbed Poppy a cherry coke.

'That will be 3 pounds girls.' I grab my card out of my phone case and tapped it on the scanner. I smiled and handed Poppy her sugary fattening drink.

'I feel dizzy can we go outside?' I mentioned.

'Yeah okay,' Poppy said in a soft, concerned voice.

We stand on the cracked concrete with burned out soggy cigs scattered around the path. We sit on a cold metal bench with green peeling paint. Poppy reaches into her pink fluffy jacket and pulls out two cigarettes and handed me one.

'Can I have one?' asked Josh. I fixed my slumped tired posture and crossed my legs.

'Sure!' Poppy said joyfully. My leg was trembling.

'You, okay?' Poppy asked.

'Oh yeah, just had too much coffee . . .' I said with a nervous chuckle. I hold my legs down with my cold pale hands. It begins to rain.

'For god's sake,' Poppy said, groaning while covering her fried straightened hair. She grabs my arm while running inside the warm crowded canteen.

'Fuck, my hair . . .' I was lightly stroking my scalp. Poppy nudged my head forward to see my hair extension tracks sliding out tugging my natural hair.

'Girl lets go the toilet,' she gasped.

'Okay,' I said in a soft relieved voice.

Poppy pushes the heavy girl's bathroom door; we get a wave of sweet vape smoke in our faces and strong cheap perfume. Poppy pushes gossiping girls out the way to get to the mirror where a few girls were fixing and reapplying their makeup. Poppy pushes me near the mirror.

'Just remove the top tracks and dry 'em,' she said with her hand on my shoulder while pulling out a pink glittery brush. I unclip my hair extensions covering my thin stringy hair and wiggle them under the hand dryer.

'Give me your brush,' I told Poppy. She hands me the brush and accidentally scratches me with her dangerous nails. I brush through the frizzy extensions then Poppy helps me clip them back. She sighs and says, 'As long as they're not visible its fine,' while getting her cheap vanilla perfume out of her bag. I role my eyes and grab the diet coke out my bag.

'I'm gonna pee really quick then go home,' Poppy stated. I smiled while leaning against the cracked wall. 'Hanna do you want to come mine and plan this party!' Poppy said obnoxiously loud over the toilet cubicle.

'Oh my god yeah, just stop yelling . . .' I replied grumpily. Poppy chuckles.

'Okay let's go,' I said as she opens the door and rushes to the sink to wash her hands. We walk down the busy corridor with boys punching each other and girls squealing, I look at Poppy and smirk. 'Jesus . . .' we both said while chuckling.

Acknowledgements

Writing this book has been a journey made possible by the encouragement, support, and inspiration of many people. Thank you to the team at Penguin Michael Joseph and to Ruth Cairns for turning the dream of writing a book into a reality.

First, I would like to thank my family. To my mum, Alisha and Wes, your unwavering belief in me and your constant support gave me the strength to push through the most challenging and emotional moments.

I would like to take this opportunity to show my gratitude to all of those who throughout my life, have inspired me, been kind to me, had faith in me, even when I wasn't the easiest to stand by. You all know who you are, even if we're not in touch anymore, please know that I will always hold you in my thoughts and my heart.

I owe a great debt to Gay Longworth, not only for your invaluable expertise, patience, and dedication. But for holding space for me when I told you my story through a tsunami of tears.

To the readers. I am deeply grateful to have the opportunity to share my winding path of life and motherhood with you. I hope you take from this book that no matter how hard life gets, there is always a brighter future over the horizon. We are stronger than we think, and love conquers all.

Finally, thank you to Brianna. You taught me so much in your short life. I will be forever grateful for the time I had with you; from the moment you came into the world to the moment you left. I hope you know how much I love you. You were my world and always will be – It's all for you Bree. I love you, goodnight xx

Esther Ghey